No More Hippos!

A Memoir of Hope for Wives Whose Husbands
Struggle with Pornography or Sexual Addiction

KOLINDA KING DUER

WestBow
PRESS

Scripture taken from the HOLY BIBLE, NEW INTERNATIONAL VERSION®. Copyright © 1973, 1978, 1984 Biblica.

Used by permission of Zondervan. All rights reserved.

WestBow Press books may be ordered through booksellers or by contacting:

WestBow Press
A Division of Thomas Nelson
1663 Liberty Drive
Bloomington, IN 47403
www.westbowpress.com
1-(866) 928-1240

Because of the dynamic nature of the Internet, any Web addresses or links contained in this book may have changed since publication and may no longer be valid. The views expressed in this work are solely those of the author and do not necessarily reflect the views of the publisher, and the publisher hereby disclaims any responsibility for them.

ISBN: 978-1-4497-0129-1 (sc)
ISBN: 978-1-4497-0130-7 (hc)
ISBN: 978-1-4497-0128-4 (e)

Library of Congress Control Number: 2010928765

Printed in the United States of America

WestBow Press rev. date: 9/10/2010

Dedication

This book is dedicated first and foremost to women from all walks of life who love their husbands and yet know there is something wrong in their marriages as a result of pornography. It is for seekers of truth who hold onto hope that their marriages will find healing and restoration through honesty, courage, and the love of Jesus Christ.

To the addict and the spouse I offer my prayers and respect as you search for answers and recover from the effects of pornography on your lives, marriages, and families. I also pray that this book will breathe life into the poor in spirit and will open eyes to Christ's hope and healing in the midst of circumstances.

****

To Tom, thank you for choosing to wrestle with these difficult issues and to fight for our marriage. You have become my knight in shining armor and I love you more now than I ever dreamed possible. Your love for Jesus shines and I have been amazed to see him at work in your life over the last six years.

To my precious girls Elizabeth, Alyssa and Victoria, I pray you will find your completeness in Jesus Christ alone so that if any man wants to marry you, he'll have come to Christ as his first love too because that's where your heart will be.

Contents

Preface

My heart's desire in writing this book is to offer hope and healing to those who find themselves in a similar situation, who are seeking answers, and who want restoration in their marriages. My intent is neither to expose anyone nor to bring shame to the addict but to offer a new beginning through the power of Jesus Christ. The resources listed in the back of this book are there for additional help.

I pray that God will take this offering and use it for His glory.

Acknowledgments

I have so many wonderful people in my life that I want to thank.

First, my heavenly Father; my Savior and Lord, Jesus Christ; and the Holy Spirit who live in me, breathing truth, life, and light into the empty places.

To Mom and Dad, for the godly heritage you gave to me. You gave me a foundation built upon the truths of God's word, which is better than any material thing of this world. You have always been such a source of encouragement to my life and I hope you know just how much I love you both. Thanks for helping to pay for the editing of this book. You are such great examples of generous and unconditional love. I am blessed to have you as my parents.

Grandma Lloyd for being an example of God's love. You showed me what it looks like to pour out one's life for others. You are an amazing person and I pray I'll be as much of a Light for Christ as you are at the age of 96!

Valerie Perley and Margaret Reid, my prayer warrior friends, who have been with me on this project since the beginning. Thanks for all of your prayers and encouragement! You are amazing!

Scott Crews, computer and technology friend, who set up the website for www.safehaven4women.com. Thanks for bartering out cakes for your computer knowledge!

To my editors: Margaret, Valerie, Tom and Tyra–Thank you!

Finally, the dear, sweet women in the Safe Haven support groups in Tennessee. Your courage, inner strength, unconditional love and perseverance I admire. I have seen Jesus in you. You are so precious to me and have filled my life with hope and such joy. I pray this book will be a source of inspiration and encouragement to you as you relish the truth that you are dearly loved by your "heavenly husband" whose love will last throughout eternity!

Introduction

It's Monday just past noon. The sunshine is streaming through the mandarin, lemon, and pomegranate leaves. I've taken the last bite of my favorite gourmet, fast food sandwich and am trying hard not to spill any crumbs on the car's seat as my husband and I head to a meeting that he will be attending. My husband, Tom, is devouring his pizza as he maneuvers our car into the parking lot of a local Methodist church. He finishes, gives me a hug and a kiss, and goes into a men's meeting that he attends at every opportunity.

He goes, because the meetings are "life" to him and to our marriage. The source of encouragement he has found in them and because of them has changed our lives in immeasurable ways. Without the fellowship of the members and the unconditional acceptance he has found, Tom would not be married to me anymore. You see, my husband is a recovering addict from pornography. I'm so proud of him and of the commitment he has made to himself, to us, and to our family.

I'm equally proud of the strength I've found, with God's help and from other women, to find healing in my own life from the effects of pornography. It is my prayer that through this book and its resources you will see that **you are not alone.** I want to offer hope that is based on the firm foundation of Jesus Christ and the strength only he can give. May you find healing that will give you the freedom to walk each day as God sees you: a beloved masterpiece, accepted and loved completely.

To walk each day from the perspective of how God sees us is possible—I know. I have learned this and can testify that with God's abundant help you, too, can be free from the effects of pornography in your marriage. It is neither easy nor fun, and yes, you will shed tears, but I promise when it is all said and done, your "heavenly husband," Jesus, will be holding your hand. With his strength and your willingness to see your situation through God's perspective, you will stand tall once again. I cannot promise that your spouse's addiction will end. I cannot promise that he will *choose* to get help. I can promise, however, that by learning how to face the hippos in your life you can walk in the Truth that will set you free. It is by the power of Christ and a willing attitude on your part that you can live a more abundant life. The choice is yours. Do you *want* to be well?

This is my story—our story. It is not fancy and, at times, it is not pretty, but nonetheless, it is the road I have traveled and am traveling. I do not know what each day will bring, but I have learned who holds each day and who will hold my tomorrows. It is because of what God has taught me through his Word and, most of all, through his consistent and faithful love in the midst of my circumstances that I share my story.

The Spirit of the Sovereign Lord
is on me, because the Lord has
anointed me to preach good news
to the poor. He has sent me to bind
up the brokenhearted, to proclaim
freedom for the captives and release
from darkness for the prisoners, to
proclaim the year of the Lord's favor
and the day of vengeance of our
God, to comfort all who mourn,
and provide for those who grieve in
Zion – to bestow on them a crown
of beauty instead of ashes, the oil of
gladness instead of mourning, and a
garment of praise instead of a spirit
of despair. They will be called oaks of
righteousness, a planting of the Lord
for the display of his splendor.

(Isaiah 61:1-3)

Part 1: My Life

"In my work with spouses I have found there is one thing they have in common: they long for their husbands to really understand the pain they are feeling as a result of their husbands' acting out. Unfortunately, it seems to be one of the last pieces for the addict to realize. Empathy doesn't come easily for most addicts. So what the spouse hopes for, and feels is imperative for her healing, is the last to come. And in this dark and frustrating place begins the journey.

I remember long ago when I was discussing a conflict I was having with my husband someone pointed out to me that my husband wasn't the obstacle. I remember that so clearly and the defensiveness I felt. I didn't think my husband was "the obstacle". Then God completed the sentence"...not only is he NOT the obstacle...he is the vehicle." "The vehicle, Lord?" "Yes, because his NOT being who you want or even who you sometimes need him to be, drives you to your knees, and thus to ME!"

This is a challenging idea to embrace because the spouse feels so hurt, disappointed and betrayed. There is an unconscious belief that if I were just married to someone who really loved me then all would be right with the world. In that way, my spouse is the vehicle that God sometimes uses to get my attention that I have somehow gotten off the path and lost my way.

The journey requires disregarding the other person altogether (or as much as is humanly possible) and begin to focus on yourself. The connection begins with self, with God and then with others. The journey requires me to begin looking at my own feelings, needs and wants. In so many addict/coaddict relationships there is the dynamic of an overfunctioning spouse and an underfunctioning addict. It is a marriage that works for a time. However, the potential gift in this heartache called addiction is that we get to rediscover ourselves and learn how to have a relationship with ourselves. From this place there is an opportunity to begin to show up in our marriage and in our other relationships in a way that is present, richer and if we are fortunate, truly intimate."

-Lisa Gohmann, Licensed Professional Counselor,
Certified Clinical Sexual Addiction Specialist

1
HIPPO 1

My earliest memories take me back to the poultry farm where my family lived in Southern Illinois from the 1960's through the 80's. On the 125-acre expanse were five chicken houses that held over 180,000 baby chickens. The long lane to our house was lined on both sides with trees and brush that grew up wild except for the weekly mowing job my dad provided during the warm summer months. The first home I lived in was a small, white house that stood just off the second curve of our lane. Modest as it was, that house was home to about half of my childhood memories. I learned how to ice skate and catch bluegill fish from the pond that glistened as the sun's rays kissed it. My Dad managed this farm that was nestled near the woods with a creek that flowed gently behind our house.

I was born the youngest of three children to God-fearing parents who believed in hard work, honesty and respecting your elders. My maiden name was King and many times I was reminded to mind my manners because I was a child of THE King Jesus.

My older sister, brother and I learned the value of honoring life and of making the most of each day because we believed that each day was a gift from God. The farm was the classroom where we learned these things and where these foundational principles were laid.

Like a finely woven tapestry, music was a strong thread sewn into the fabric of my life. I remember my Mom waking me up almost every morning as she played the upright piano near my bedroom in the basement of our house. She would serenade my sleepy lids and awaken my ears to Gospel songs that she sang and played with passion. My Dad's idea of getting us kids up each morning consisted of a drill sergeant's methods including sprinkling us with water and bellowing, "Time to get up!" while he shocked our nervous systems awake by switching on the overhead light. For some strange reason, he thought it was funny, a point I still don't fully comprehend to this day.

We were the first students picked up by the school bus every morning at not a minute past 7:25 and the last ones let off every afternoon around 4:30. We rode that bus every day for an hour, each way. Our bus driver was one of the most cantankerous people you would ever want to meet. Somehow all three of us lived through her capricious temperaments. We always knew if she was in a mood if she stared at us in the overhead mirror above her steering wheel. Her beady eyes would peer up sneakily over the rims of her old glasses. She loved to hit every bone-jarring hole on the old country roads and almost seemed to smile with glee, as our small bodies would be catapulted upward and plopped downward after each bump.

We lived about 4 miles from the nearest town, a blink of an eye populous with an old Methodist church that sat juxtaposed to the railroad tracks. The road coming into that town propelled your car, first to the right, then over the old tracks, and then immediately to the left. Just off the main thoroughfare, was the one road I traveled more than a thousand times. It was nicknamed "Bumpy Hollow," a stretch of road that jostled every bit of life out of you if you drove down it even the slightest bit over the speed limit of 35. I didn't live in the tiny town, but rather drove through it to get to our farm almost every day. These Norman Rockwell memories are a menagerie reminding me of where I came from, a warm and tender picture in my mind's eye of the childhood I was blessed to call "mine."

My parents were both gifted singers, and played musical instruments. Some of my dearest memories are of family sings where we would circle the piano while Mom tickled the ivory and Dad would lead us in songs that seemed to touch Heaven. As soon as my sister, brother and I were old enough to sit up, we were privy to listening to Southern Gospel and Gospel music led by the greats of that time: The Rambos and Hemphills, to name a few. By the time I was two and a half, I could sing "He Touched Me" solo, much to my parents' joy.

It was from these experiences that I found acceptance and admiration from listeners by using my God-given talent of singing. No longer was I only the "baby" of the King family, I was a gifted and much-admired singer. Our family sang as often as we could in local churches, at revivals, campground meetings and even in the public school once for a PTO meeting. For me, singing became my identity and a source of strength. Like the runner in the movie, *The Chariots of Fire*, when I sang, I felt God's pleasure.

By the time I was 18, I had an ego the size of Montana and I, like most teenagers, thought I could do anything – without consequences. Before I finished my senior year of high school, I began dating a guy named "Bob." I was only 18 at the time and met him through a mutual friend. He was an exciting guy, one who had boatloads of confidence. Looking back now, I would call it arrogance, but from my naïve perspective, he looked really cool!

"Bob" lived in a trailer with his dear grandfather for whom he had no respect and of whom he took full advantage. He was a guy who loved to live in the fast lane and, truthfully, his life was alluring to the quiet, protected childhood I had experienced. We dated at the end of my senior year and became "boyfriend and girlfriend."

After dating for about 4 months, our relationship had grown to a place where I honestly had started to fall in love with him. One night I stopped by to visit him and his grandpa was not home. It was late and I dropped in for what I thought would be a quick visit. "Bob" was not his normal self and seemed agitated. I remember trying to find out what was going on, but his anger was apparent. I could smell alcohol on his breath and decided to leave. I started to go and he grabbed me by my arm. I was shaken and immediately felt scared by his actions. He had never before been in any way violent or abusive, but this time was different. In a matter of minutes, he pushed me violently to the ground. He was on top of me and was hurting me. I remember feeling completely numb and utterly shocked that someone I thought cared about me would violate me. When it was over, I gathered up my ripped clothes, dried my tears as best I could and ran out the door. I don't remember much after that, only that I cried myself to sleep feeling abandoned, rejected and utterly dirty. I didn't have the inner strength or the self-respect to tell anyone. Shame came over me like a heavy blanket and I suddenly felt the need to hide what had happened, a mistake I have regretted every since.

It was shortly after this incident that he broke up with me. I remember trying to sort it all out in my wounded heart. Somehow there had to be some sense in all of this, but there wasn't. In my mind, I kept on trying to fix it, to somehow find a way to make it all better, but I couldn't. Instead, I blamed myself for his actions thinking maybe if I had just done something different or had been a better girlfriend. It never occurred to me to call the police or tell my dad and mom who would have undoubtedly taken full care of the situation. I had every right to get help, but I didn't. I just pulled all of the pain inside, trying to pretend it didn't hurt and that it really wasn't all THAT bad.

The energy I exerted trying to hide my shame and pain from the rape became a sort of hippo that I knew was present but that I chose to pretend didn't matter. I knew that wrong had taken place and that I needed to address the issue, but out of fear, I chose instead to bury it in hopes that by denying the pain, it would somehow magically disappear. This was the first hippo in my life. I named this one, "tainted and defective" and quickly put a nice pink tablecloth over it, hoping no one would notice, especially me.

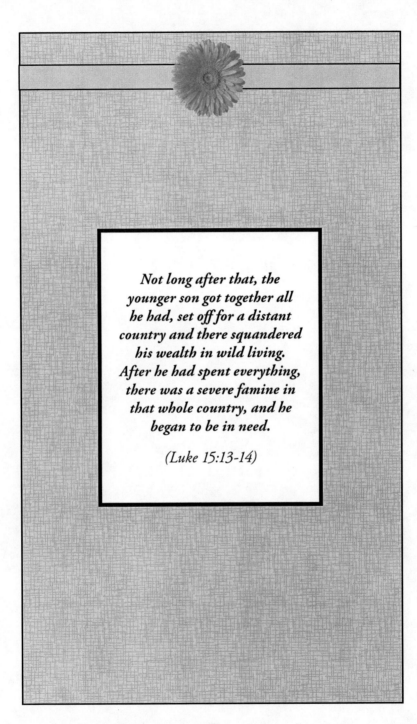

Not long after that, the younger son got together all he had, set off for a distant country and there squandered his wealth in wild living. After he had spent everything, there was a severe famine in that whole country, and he began to be in need.

(Luke 15:13-14)

2
LIVIN' ON MY OWN

After I turned 19, my parents moved from the farm in Illinois to work for my uncle in Texas. For the first time in my life, I lived on my own and made my own money to pay for bills. I lived in a run-down trailer park in the southern part of town and thought I had really made it! I was working full time as a computer data entry operator for an auto-parts company and with the meager leftovers from my paycheck, was able to have somewhat of a social life.

Like a lot of small towns, the big highlight of the weekend was to go out with friends and play pool in the local bar. My best friend, Denise, and I used to go out and drink a little and thought, at the time, that hangin' with the rowdy crowd was a cool thing to do. I dated a few guys. One in particular was worse for me than a canker sore, but I was in denial about where my life was heading and continued going out with him anyway. All the while, though, I knew deep down that God's hand was guiding me and that his Spirit was wooing me back to obedience. I was like the prodigal son who knew he was running from God's best for his life, but I just kept on running.

I worked, paid my monthly bills, and pretty much "existed" for about eight months, until I hit rock bottom. One Sunday afternoon I drove to my brother and sister-in-law's house, which was twenty-five miles away. As I headed out of town, I heard my car gurgle and sputter.

I coasted off to the side of the road only to see that I was out of gas. Out of gas! I had no money in my bank account and was living paycheck to paycheck. I was sick, tired, lonely, and just plain fed up with the way my life was going. I walked to a nearby gas station where, thankfully, they had a gas can they would let me borrow. I wrote a bad check, because I didn't have a credit card, and I was on my way. When I got to my brother's house I told him and his wife about my troubles and they graciously gave me twenty dollars, which to me at that time felt like one-hundred dollars.

Right after the gasoline incident, I went to our favorite local bar that my friends and I had frequented to play pool and have some "fun." After coming out after midnight and noticing the long line of cars that framed the parking lot to my left, I saw something sparkle as the moon's beams hit them. Then, I began seeing more and more of the pieces creating a prism of crystal both on the ground and on the hoods of the cars. Then, to my horror, I saw my car and those next to it and realized that someone had taken a ball bat to not only our front windshields but also to the side windows. Vandals had broken my windshield, side window, and front headlights. I called the police, who towed my vehicle away to the repair shop and had to mooch off my friends for a week for rides while repairs were being made. For me, this night was symbolic of how my life had become. I was broken, spent, and frankly, needed repair.

It was from this point that I began to rethink my life and some of the absolutely horrible choices I had been making. All the while, I could hear the gentle, soft voice of God in my mind and knew he still loved me regardless of the disobedience in my life. I felt him calling me back to himself. He used circumstances like having an "empty" tank and allowing one of my worldly possessions to be "broken" to draw me near to his presence again. With all the courage I could muster, I began to call out to God for help, asking him to show me how to get back on track.

I began recalling some of the childhood verses I had memorized at Vacation Bible School and in Sunday school class:

- "Be still and *know* that I am God." (Psalm 46:10a; italics added)

- "He who began a good work in you will carry it on to completion." (Philippians 1:6b)

- "But seek *first* his kingdom...." (Matthew 6:33a; italics added)

- "For *all* have sinned and fall short of the glory of God, and are justified freely by his grace through the redemption that came by Christ Jesus." (Romans 3:23; italics added)

- "Therefore, there is now *no* condemnation for those who are in Christ Jesus, because through Christ Jesus the law of the Spirit of life set me free from the law of sin and death." (Romans 8:1-2; italics added)

- "No temptation has seized you except what is common to man. And God is faithful; he will not let you be tempted beyond what you can bear. But when you are tempted, he will also *provide a way out* so that you can stand up under it." (1 Corinthians 10:13; italics added)

Something inside of me began to change—to turn from the way I was going—and to cause me to walk in a new way. The Word says, "If anyone is in Christ, he is a *new* creature; the old has gone, the *new* has come." (2 Corinthians 5:17, emphasis mine[1]) God began to do a new work in me. His Spirit, who had been gently calling to me throughout my disobedient years, began to freely work in my life. I began listening to him instead of running from him. Though I still kept the first hippo buried in the recesses of my heart under its blanket of shame, I slowly began turning my life over to God and seeking him first again.

Within a month, I sold my car, gave my notice at the trailer park where I had been living, and made arrangements to meet my wonderful sister in Austin, Texas, where we would travel to Del Rio, where my parents lived. The plan was to surprise my parents who I knew would be ecstatic that I was moving back home. My dear auntie volunteered to go with me and help with the driving. I felt like she was my guardian angel, carrying me from the desert to the Promised Land.

---

1 "emphasis mine" or "emphasis added" means the author has either italicized, capitalized or made bold parts of text for emphasis

*But while he was still a long way off,
his father saw him and was filled
with compassion for him; he ran to
his son, threw his arms around him
and kissed him…But the father said
to his servants, "Quick! Bring the best
robe and put it on him. Put a ring
on his finger and sandals on his feet.
Bring the fattened calf and kill it.
Let's have a feast and celebrate. For
this son of mine was dead and is alive
again; he was lost and is found."
So they began to celebrate.*

(Luke 15:20b, 22-24)

3
TEXAS AND TOM

It was in January of 1984 that I moved from the dumpy trailer park to Del Rio, Texas, to live with my parents again. I was not quite 20 years old at the time. Like the story of the prodigal son, my parents' arms were open wide, welcoming me with more authentic love than I had felt in a long time. No condemnation, just acceptance, tons of homemade food, and a nice warm bed to sleep in for as long as I needed.

I soon acclimated to the warmer weather of Texas and found a job and began working for a lawyer as a legal secretary. I discovered, to my delight, life in Del Rio to be quite fun. The weather was unbelievably hot but absolutely perfect for getting a great tan. I loved being near my family again, which included my grandparents, some wonderful aunts, uncles, and cousins. It didn't take me long to meet some handsome pilots in training, as the Air Force Base was nearby. It was a golden time in my life, you know, when you feel like you have the world by the tail! I was young, fancy free, and full of hope. I met a nice pilot and we dated about six months before he "washed out" of the pilot program. He ended up leaving Texas and moving back to New York. It was a sad time for me, so I kept busy by working full time and hangin' with my friends.

It was shortly after this that I made a good friend. She was a lot of fun and, together, we made some good memories. We kept it "clean" and I began to learn how to have fun again without jeopardizing my values. Life for me began to feel good again. I began to read my Bible daily and to seek God's will for my life, instead of listening to everybody else's opinion.

It was Halloween night of 1985 that my romantic life changed forever. My friend, Mary, talked me into going to a costume party. The prospect of going out that night was a dismal thought to me, as it had only been a month since I had broken up with the pilot. My friend was persuasive, however, and after stuffing my bib overalls with straw and applying rosy, red lipstick to my cheeks, Mary and I went to the party. On the way, though, she decided to stop by her friend's apartment. He was in the Air Force and shared the place with two other pilots.

I walked in and saw a good-looking guy lying on the couch. His feet were propped up on the armrest opposite his head, a magazine was in his hands, and he was watching a football game on the small 19 inch TV, which, by the way, was a big-screen TV back in the 80s! I thought he was cute but the prospect of dating another pilot or any man of any stature, station, or kind totally nauseated me. I was done with dating, sick of guys, and didn't want any kind of relationship. Mary introduced us and that was that —nothing more, nothing less.

A little while later, we left the apartment and went on to the Halloween party. After about forty-five minutes of being "hit on" by less than desirable males, I wanted to leave, so we did. My friend suggested we go back to see what her friends at the apartment were up to. Tom, the cute guy I had met earlier, was the only one hanging around the place when we arrived, so we invited him to go and play putt-putt golf with us. It was fun, yet I couldn't for the life of me get him to talk. He was horribly shy, in my gregarious opinion, which was something that baffled me! I later found out that he thought I was married and didn't want to flirt with a married woman. That was admirable, I thought.

Two months passed and I saw Tom again at the Air Force's Wings Ceremony where the class assignments were given. The event was the culmination of the 1-year training Tom had gone through and was anticipated by all the pilots. I had gone with some of my friends and was enjoying the festivities of the evening. (Ah, there's nothing like a man in uniform!) I saw Tom. He walked toward me and I smiled. As he passed by, he acted nonchalant and didn't even smile back at me! My pride was a bit wounded, but I thought, "Oh, well. You can't win them all!"

A few weeks later, my friend, Mary, who worked with my Mom at the Karmelkorn Shop® at the mall called and asked if I wanted to go to a party at her friend's apartment where we had met Tom. I remember walking in and being overwhelmed by the group of rowdy partiers. Front and center was Tom who was playing a makeshift guitar. He was using an old wooden clock, and was strumming the once vertical shaft of the clock, getting down to the music. "He's not only incredibly shy," I thought, "he's also a little weird."

I know God must sit on His throne and laugh and laugh at my thought processes sometimes. I say this because later that very night, Tom and I began talking amongst the crowd of people in that very small apartment. We ended up going into his bedroom and just sitting and talking. What is funny is that we didn't "make out" like most people would think. I actually began sharing my faith in Jesus Christ with him and told him how very important God was to me. I shared how I had made some very bad choices while living on my own and how I knew God had called me back to a place of being in a right relationship with him. I shared how I didn't ever want to go back to living the way I had been living.

After we had been in his bedroom talking for over an hour, it occurred to both of us that we should go back out into the party. I was mortified at the thought of entering the living room again because I knew what most people would be thinking. I told Tom this and he, being the gentleman that he was, had a brilliant idea. We could climb out the window onto the small roof below and hop down to the first floor...so we did! I laughed and laughed first of all, because we were so sneaky and second of all, because it was just plain fun to be doing something so adventurous!

About a week later, my phone rang and it was Tom. His kind but nervous voice greeted me as he reminded me of who he was, recounting our rooftop adventure. We talked that night for more than forty-five minutes. Finally, I couldn't stay awake any longer and asked him if there was anything in particular that he wanted. He nervously went on to ask me out for an "official" date for the following Friday night.

The week seemed to creep by in slow motion until Friday finally came. Tom came to pick me up and I was immediately impressed by how much of a gentleman he was. He opened my car door and all entry doors and wowed me when he pulled out my chair for me at our table. He was gentle and kind—qualities unfamiliar to me from some of my former suitors. We were just getting to know each other and I liked the first impressions of this quiet, young man in the pilot's suit.

Over the course of the next few weeks, we dated regularly. I remember I was taking a psychology class at the time at a community college nearby. I had written a paper called "The Effects of Pornography on Our Society" and showed it to Tom. Being the naïve, pollyanna person that I was, I thought nothing of the ashen face he had as he read my scathing observation of this issue. I ranted and raged about how awful I thought the whole thing was and how it ruins lives and destroys marriages, not to mention how it degrades women. I didn't think anything of the nonchalant way he handed me the paper and just said, "Good." I didn't think for a minute that this issue might be something he struggled with.

It was a few weeks later that Tom got orders to go to an instructor school about three hours away in San Antonio. Try as I may, I couldn't help but have strong feelings for him. He was handsome, charming, gentle spirited, a little quieter than I liked, but that allowed me to just talk and talk and talk some more! He was a pilot and had a great career ahead of him. I was thinking, "good catch!" The pieces of the puzzle were all coming together just as I had dreamed they would, but then something happened that made me wonder....

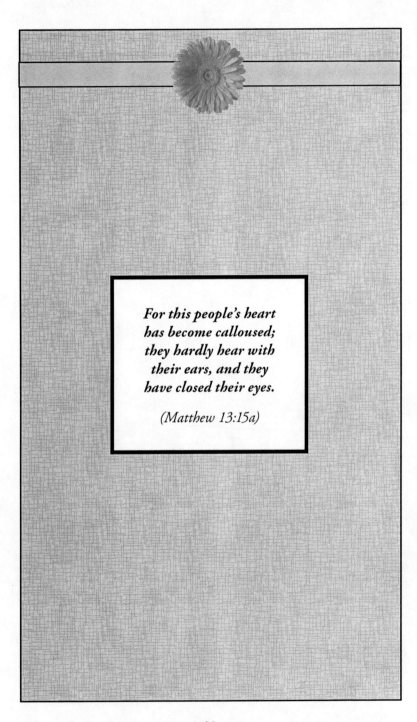

*For this people's heart
has become calloused;
they hardly hear with
their ears, and they
have closed their eyes.*

(Matthew 13:15a)

4
HIPPO 2

It was sometime in the early spring months of 1986 that Tom had to pack up his apartment belongings and move into the base apartments en route to San Antonio for his training. I had gone over to the apartment to help him load up his things. It was late and I remember lying down on Tom's bed and napping while he and his roommate worked in the next room. I was half asleep when they both came in to retrieve more stuff. As his friend moved something under the bed, he snickered. Tom snickered too, and I heard him reach for something under the bed and take it out with him.

I thought, "'wonder what that was all about?" I didn't say anything to Tom about it. I didn't want to know. It was easier to stick my head in the sand like an ostrich rather than confront the situation. So I said nothing and tried to stuff my premonitions way down deep in hopes that they would not come true any time in the near future. I honestly didn't suspect it was porn, though my heart knew something wasn't kosher.

I wrestled with questions but discounted the incident as no big deal. I wanted what I wanted —a husband—and, in making my choice, I chose not to put my big girl britches on and deal. I was a coward and I knew it; I wasn't willing to confront my fears and ask the hard questions. If I had asked him, I may have found out the truth, and, then again, maybe not, but at least I would have been proactive instead of reactive. If I had dared, I could have probably saved myself a lot of pain—but I didn't. I chose to hide another hippo in the recesses of my heart, covering it up along with the others from my teenage years that my heart dared not face.

The following week, Tom left for training. On the day he left, he sent me an African violet with a note on it that said, "I'll Miss You. Love, Tom." My heart skipped a beat as I knew that all of my attempts to buffer my feelings for this guy were going to be futile. I thought, "This one is different from all of the others." So I held the plant in my arms and twirled around like Cinderella in the foyer of the castle, dreaming of her prince.

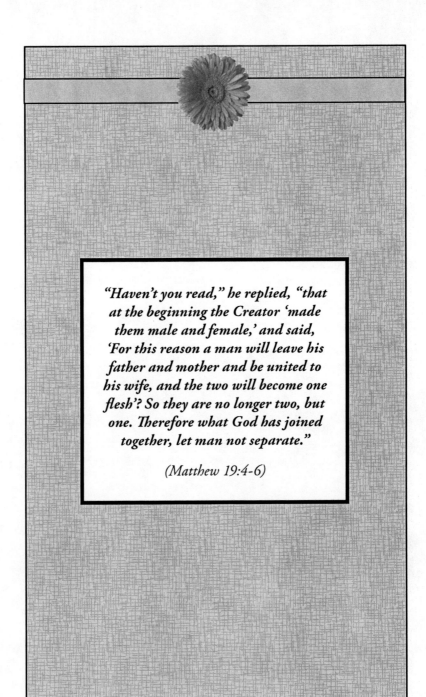

"Haven't you read," he replied, "that at the beginning the Creator 'made them male and female,' and said, 'For this reason a man will leave his father and mother and be united to his wife, and the two will become one flesh'? So they are no longer two, but one. Therefore what God has joined together, let man not separate."

(Matthew 19:4-6)

5
Proposal & Wedding Day

It was May 16, Tom's birthday. It had been two months since I had tucked away my second hippo that maybe there was something I needed to address. I dismissed the premonitions I had as nothing more than silliness. We continued dating and both of our hearts were falling in love. Tom had finished his training in San Antonio and had moved back to Del Rio. On this particular night, I was waiting for him to pick me up for our Friday date. He came to the door looking as handsome as ever. After the usual public display of affection, I grabbed his birthday gifts and gave them to him to open. I thought he was acting "weird," but I didn't know what was up. Never did I imagine he was just biding his time to ask me to marry him.

We left my parents' home and went over to his apartment and watched a movie. It was around midnight when he awoke me from my slumber. I had fallen asleep on the couch with my head on his lap. He shook my shoulder and said, "Kolinda, I want to talk to you. I want to talk to you about our relationship and where we are going. I have been doing a lot of thinking about us."

At this point, I woke up and wondered where the conversation was going. Earlier that week, we had talked about the future and what each of us wanted it to look like. I remember feeling scared that either the relationship wouldn't work out or that, gosh, maybe it would and then what? I could see the seriousness in Tom's eyes and heard it in his voice. I sat up and he said, "I love you. Will you marry me?" He put a small velvet box in my hand and I remember thinking, "Say something! He just proposed! This is it: the white picket fence! It's 'The Question' you've been waiting for—the knight in shining armor is asking you to take his hand in marriage! Say something! This is your chance to finally wear that poncho with the red pompoms for real!" My mind raced back to my childhood school days at recess when my friends and I would play the "Mommy Game." The object was to be the lucky one who got to wear a colorful poncho my Mom had made and be Mommy for the day. The coveted covering with the red pompoms signified the dream each of us had of marrying and of being a Mom. Here I was, 21 years old, and finally, it was my turn! For the first time in my life, I had to force my mouth to open not because I didn't want to marry him, but because I was completely blown over! I finally was able to articulate, "Yes!"

The wedding plans were immediately put into play as the clock was ticking for a September 6 wedding. We both worked feverishly over the weeks that ensued and by the time the day came, all the details for our special day were finished. I wish I could say that the day of the wedding was sunny and that there was a soft, warm breeze greeting our guests, but I can't. The rain came down in buckets and the wind blew everyone's skirts and pants to their legs. It didn't matter to me, though. I was so happy to be marrying my knight and those who dared brave the torrential downpour came and shared in our day. It went off without a hitch, and, by the time we finished the ceremony, the rain had subsided and the sun began to shine. We spent our honeymoon night at a nice, local hotel. The next day, we drove southwest for a week in the sun and sand.

We stayed at a condo on the shores of South Padre Island just off the southern tip of Texas. It was a perfect time to be there as all of the Labor Day throngs had dissipated and the beach was virtually ours. Our condo was beautiful and the palm trees that bordered our pool reminded us that we were truly in an island paradise. I honestly think we could have honeymooned anyplace—hung a hammock between two trees in the back yard—and it would have felt like a paradise to me. I was in love with Tom, so in love that everything else seemed to fade into oblivion. I had met the man of my dreams and nothing could take away my happiness.

I woke up the second morning to find Tom gone. I was curious and waited for about an hour for his return. When he returned, he told me that he had gone to find a newspaper. I remember feeling uneasy. In reality, I believed in my heart of hearts that the pink foot of the second hippo was sticking out of the closet. The wedding ring was on my finger. I was married to this man and all of a sudden I was wishing I had had the courage and the emotional health to ask the hard questions about that night we moved him onto the base. It was too late, though, I thought. So, I stuffed the pink foot of my hippo back in the closet, swallowed hard, and quietly shut the door.

But Ruth replied, "Don't urge
me to leave you or to turn
back from you. Where you go
I will go, and where you
stay I will stay. Your people
will be my people and
your God my God."

(Ruth 1:16a)

6
DEUTSCHLAND!

W e had been married only two short months when Tom got new orders from the Air Force to go to Germany. Germany? I couldn't believe it! I had never been to any foreign country before and the prospect of moving so far away from all that I knew and held dear was exciting yet daunting.

Before we could head across "the big pond," our material possessions had to be packed by the Air Force. The movers came and loaded up our small apartment's belongings. We didn't have much, just love, but that seemed like enough at the time. We moved to temporary housing on base and waited for our departure date.

On November 18, 1986, we boarded a plane that took off for Germany. It was nighttime and I remember looking out the window of the plane onto the vast canvas of the speckled lights below us. Suddenly, as our plane headed east, the captain came over the intercom and said, "Well, folks, as you look down, you'll see the border of the eastern coast of the United States." I could see the familiar shape that is common on so many maps and then, suddenly, there was darkness below us as black as tar. We were soaring over the Atlantic Ocean some forty thousand feet above its surface with billions of gallons of water below us, and there was nothing for me to do but sit back in my seat, take a deep breath, and trust God to carry us safely to the other side.

We flew for about six hours and made a landing in Shannon, Ireland. We deplaned and had a chance to walk around the terminal, stretch our legs, and look at the shops, offering lots of green items with four-leaf clovers on them. Everywhere I looked outside was green. It was truly breathtaking. Then we boarded our plane again and headed for Frankfurt, Germany, our last stop on our very long journey.

As we landed, I thought, "Things feel different here." Walking through the airport, the signs in *Deutche* signaled the reality of where we were. Suddenly, we had to totally depend on each other and, most of all, on God, to help us through whatever we faced.

Our Air Force greeter, or sponsor as he was called, met us at Frankfurt and offered a welcomed American presence from the unfamiliarity we were experiencing. He spoke English and that was one of the greatest sounds I had heard all day. We heaved our huge suitcases into the back of his small European car and headed south toward the base or *Pflugplatz* near *Zweibrucken*. The ride took us over two hours, but would have been much longer had we not been on the *autobahn* where the slowest speed is at least sixty-five, and most drive over a hundred! To me, it was all so exciting.

Our sponsor eventually took us to the *Zwei Rosen* (Two Roses) Hotel in *Zweibrucken* for our first night's sleep. It was a historic building, rich in character. Everywhere I looked, from the intricately carved trim on the walls and doorposts to the fluffy thick duvet covers on our beds, felt German. We tried to sleep that first night, but due to jet lag, we woke up at two o'clock in the morning, thinking it was later. By week's end, we found our way to sleep and adjusted to the new time zone.

That first morning after we finally found sleep I awoke and walked over to the hotel windows and looked down on the street below. As soon as we could, we dressed and went out on the street or *pfutzgangerzone* as they call it. The only German words I knew at the time were *Guten Tag* (good day) and *Wiedersehen* (good-bye). So, every time I entered a new store, I said, "*Guten Tag!*" and waved.

And every time I left the store, I said, "*Wiedersehen!*" and waved. It worked great until a shop owner said something back that I didn't understand, and then I had that deer-in-the-headlights look all the while smiling and waving as I quickly exited the shop.

Our sponsor and his wife escorted us around the countryside in search of a place to live. They helped us find a new apartment on the bottom level of a home in a little village called *Dietrichingen*. It had two bedrooms, kitchen, large walkout living room and the luxury of a pantry. I say *luxury* because in Germany taxes are paid for every room in a house, including closets, so to have a pantry was a big deal. We were thrilled to find such a nice place. Our German landowners were very kind to us and lived on the top floor of the house.

It was beautiful there, with views of the gentle rolling hills in the distance. I learned to speak German well enough to frequent the local farmer's market each Saturday on the *Pfutzgangerzone* (foot-people zone or pedestrian zone) in *Zweibrucken*. Fresh flowers, vegetables, fruits, and handmade goods were plentiful each week. I busied my days with Air Force officers' wives' activities, meetings, and volunteer work around the base while Tom began his three year tour with the base. He flew in the European Theater in the area that consisted of Spain, Italy, England, and all over Germany.

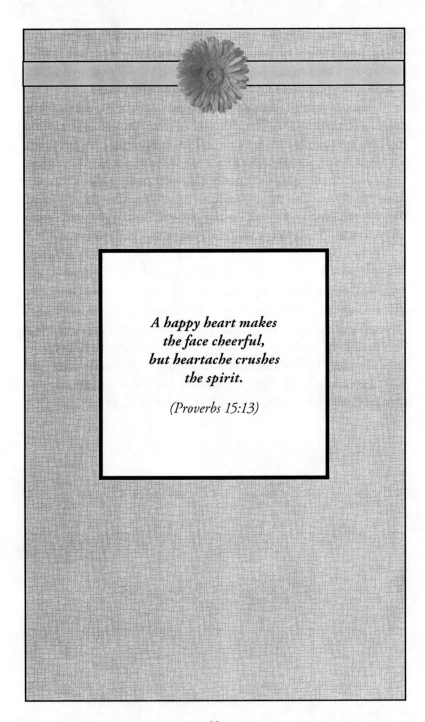

*A happy heart makes
the face cheerful,
but heartache crushes
the spirit.*

(Proverbs 15:13)

7
HIPPO 3

After Tom's training period on the C-23, he was sent on his first TDY, or Temporary Duty, to Italy (The military likes to make *everything* into an acronym!) He was only gone for three days, but it felt like thirty. When he opened the back door, I screamed and ran down the hallway and into his arms. He laughed as we embraced. He swung me around and our lips met; neither of us wanted the moment to end. I was so incredibly in love with him, so enamored with this quiet, gentle pilot. I believed he felt the same for me. I truly felt I had met the man of my dreams and that nothing could ruin our "Cinderella and Prince Charming" life.

After feasting on a lovingly prepared meal and enduring the clean-up detail that followed, it was time for bed. We both had one thing on our minds, except, for some odd reason I felt something was terribly wrong. Tom wasn't himself. There was a distance between us, a void that felt like the Grand Canyon. I looked at Tom and his face was sad. He began by saying, "I have something to tell you... something that happened on my trip that I need to tell you about." He went on to disclose his indiscretions while on his last trip. He had watched some pornographic shows on the European TV channels, had given in to fantasy, and had been emotionally unfaithful to me.

Now, for those who are not Christians, this "giving in to fantasy" is not something to feel bad about and definitely not a "sin." Jesus said in Matthew 5:27-28, "You have heard that it was said, 'Do not commit adultery.' But I tell you that anyone who looks at a woman lustfully has already committed adultery with her in his heart." As a Christian, I believe God's Word is true and that the reason there are guidelines in it is for our good. When a couple gets married and they make a promise to love, honor, and cherish the other person, then committing adultery with someone else whether it is emotional or physical is a violation of that covenant.

Tom went on to disclose a twelve year habit and compulsion he had of viewing pornography on videos, TV, and in magazines. He also went on to tell me that he had been doing these things since he was thirteen years old. He told me that he had been looking at porn magazines since that time, but since we had been married he hadn't looked at the magazines: the other things, yes, magazines, no. He believed that once he married me the compulsions to view porn would go away, but they hadn't. They had lessened, yes, but had not disappeared completely.

I remember feeling like a gale force wind had blown over me. I felt disoriented and confused. Pornography? Did you say *pornography*? My knight in shining armor was hooked on pornography? It was at this very minute that my eyes were opened and the second hippo came in to view, this time very clearly. I remembered the moving incident: the stack of "something" underneath his bed and his friend's giggles. Now there was no question in my mind as to what the stack was. I asked him, "Well, now that you are married, you can stop, right? I mean, you have everything sexually that you need, so you can stop, right?"

I remember Tom's face and the sadness in his eyes. He told me he would try and I believed he meant it. The only problem was he had been stimulating the chemicals in his brain and his physical body for more than twelve years. The idea of just quitting when he wanted to was not going to be an easy one.

The days and weeks after his revelation, I felt distant from Tom, confused, and numb. Here I was, in Germany some six thousand miles away from home, with this new realization. I felt like the foundation under my feet had been ripped away and I was floating in an abyss of confusion. I didn't know who to trust, for the one man I had totally trusted had been emotionally unfaithful. He had revealed his deepest struggle to me and I, honestly, did not know how to help him nor how to deal with the pain I was feeling inside.

If we had both possessed the skills of knowing how to speak our truths to each other, I believe a lot of our marital problems could have ended right here. If we had the emotional and spiritual maturity grounded in godly wisdom to immediately begin counseling, things could have been different. But instead of talking freely, expressing our true feelings with honesty and dealing with the issue, we chose to stick the hippopotamus back in the closet and put a lock on the door, hoping the problem would somehow fix itself. But no amount of hoping, wishing, dreaming, or praying could fix our problems. We needed so much more, but neither of us knew how to find the tools that could remedy our troubled marriage. I chose to deny and hide my feelings and, in turn, became paranoid and angry. Tom chose to hide his unfaithful choices from me and became paralyzed by shame.

Remember:
God is not the author of confusion, Satan is.

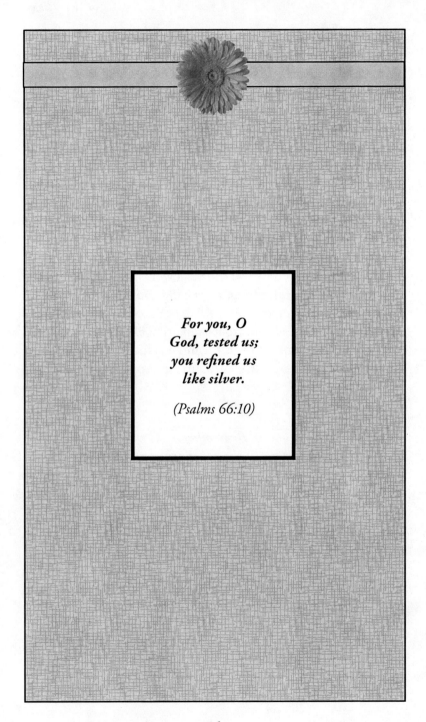

*For you, O
God, tested us;
you refined us
like silver.*

(Psalms 66:10)

8

TWO WORLDS, ONE CRAZY DANCE

(This part of our story is given by permission by my husband, Tom.)

Tom was raised in a very large and religious family; he was one of ten children. By birth, he was cast in the role of the middle child, number five. He learned at a very young age the importance of being self-sufficient, having his own paper route at the age of eight. His dad worked hard as a salesman every week and was, unfortunately, away from home Monday through Friday. His mom performed the daunting task of raising ten children, mostly alone, during the week. Though she did what to most would seem an impossible job, Tom never really received the nurturing that he needed. With so many brothers and sisters to care for, he was forced to grow up too fast and was, in many ways, abandoned. When at home, his dad did the best he could to reconnect with his ten children before leaving again each Monday morning. His parents did what all good-intentioned parents do: the very best they could with what they had and with the parenting skills they had learned from their parents.

By the time I met and married him, Tom was twenty-five and knew how to sort and do laundry better than I did! He had graduated from Notre Dame with a degree in mechanical engineering and had been trained by the Air Force. When we married, he was a master at sufficiency, at least when it came to tasks, while I, on the other hand, was a starry-eyed dreamer with visions of romantic, white-picket fences dancing in my head.

When we moved to Germany, I was clueless and, honestly, naïve about a lot of things, especially sexual addiction. So, when Tom revealed his addiction to porn, I did what most of us do when faced with something about which we know nothing. I defaulted to the practices of my childhood and began counting my blessings and praying that all of this "sinful stuff" would go away, all the while denying the reality of the hippo in our new German home.

I had many great role models growing up. From godly women who invested hours into my life through Sunday school classes, pastors and teachers who shared the Good News with me in Vacation Bible School to my dear grandparents who made sure they lived out the commandment to love and serve others before themselves. Somehow, though, I picked up a notion along the way that it wasn't safe or okay to talk about things like addiction and especially not *sexual* addiction. Maybe it was because I had watched too many episodes of *Leave It To Beaver* that I got the wrong idea that it's okay to let others know only the good stuff about our lives. Maybe it was because I was so busy trying to keep up the façade that my life, especially my marriage, was the storybook kind that I didn't speak up. Either way, denying the reality of it didn't do anyone any good.

With this belief system in place, I kept our little problem between Tom and me. I prayed and I prayed and I prayed. When I realized that wasn't producing the results I wanted, I began to query some of my friends at our church, asking them if looking at porn was "normal" in their marriages. (You know, misery loves company kind of thing.) I thought, "If everyone's doing this, then maybe it's not so bad." I got answers ranging from "Oh, yes! *Every* man does things like that. Don't worry about it. It's no biggie!" to answers like, "Oh, my gosh! That man's got a demon in him. He's possessed!" At best, the answers were shrouded in a blanket of shame and denial of the gravity of the effect it could have on the wife. Now, my already confused mind was even more perplexed. I knew one thing for sure, though:

No one in the church wanted to talk about this hippo.

I learned quickly that this issue made everyone uncomfortable. I just wanted some answers, but didn't get any that brought satisfaction to my heart.

Growing up in the church, I had learned at an early age to not question most authority over me. So, when I got the hush hush answers I did from people I trusted and looked up to in the church, I chose to hide the hippo because it was apparent to me that this issue was taboo. Out of frustration and a deep-seated lack of courage, I chose to keep my secret to myself. I didn't nag Tom about it, because I had told him in the beginning how I felt about it and assumed that would be enough. Tom's upbringing taught him a similar belief system: just keep things to yourself and it will work out one way or another, usually another, but, hey at least you will avoid a confrontation. Don't cause problems by going against the status quo. Just do whatever it takes to get along. And that is what we both did.

Even though we knew the hippo was in our home, we did our darnedest to pretend it wasn't there. Busy, busy, busy was my motto. I was involved in every officers' wives' club and church activity I could find while Tom flew his airplane all over Europe.

This crazy dance seemed to work for us for a while or so it seemed. We didn't seek professional help and thought we could bluff our way through the situation. Thankfully, though, God used some unlikely people in our lives to shake things up and to peel back some of our dysfunctional coping methods. He aligned our circumstances in such a way that what was really underneath the façade began to surface. As a silversmith uses high heat to bring the hidden dross to the surface to be discarded so the beauty of the metal can shine through, God used relational discomfort to shine his light on our core issues and to force us to see the dross that we needed to deal with. (Proverbs 25:4)

Warning: this bringing up the dross thing? It's not fun!

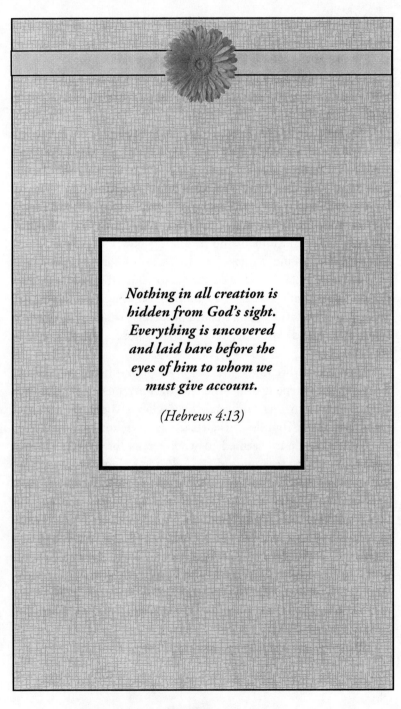

Nothing in all creation is hidden from God's sight. Everything is uncovered and laid bare before the eyes of him to whom we must give account.

(Hebrews 4:13)

9

EMOTIONAL AFFAIRS

Shortly after Tom's revelation about his compulsion, our Air Force sponsors began coming to our church. We had only been married about four months at the time and we were both still reeling from the reality of the growing hippo that seemed to take up more space in our German apartment than I wanted to admit. Unfortunately for our marriage, we didn't seek professional help with our issues, choosing instead to masquerade as if all was well.

As our sponsors continued coming to church each week, I grew increasingly uncomfortable every time they were around. The wife was a shy but attractive woman for whom Tom told me he had felt sorry. He claimed her husband wasn't very attentive to her. He was the gregarious one and she was more withdrawn. Every time we had a social event or a potluck, I would catch Tom watching her every move and paying a lot of attention to her. It got to the point that he would stare at her and hang onto her every word. It all felt so "crazy" to me, mainly because in my mind Tom was married to me in every sense of the word and shouldn't be acting this way if he truly loved me. (That's true, but he was an **addict.** Oh, and, by the way, I was **codependent,** enabling and allowing him to hurt me with his behavior by not setting down firm boundaries or speaking truth to him—more on this later!)

I felt so out of control. Like the date rape I had encountered at eighteen, I didn't know what to do with this craziness! I didn't possess the courage or wisdom to stand up for myself and scream, "Hey, you are *my* husband! I don't feel comfortable with this! I need this to stop! I need to know you are devoted to me emotionally and not to anyone else! I need you to quit spending so much emotional time with this other woman!" But I didn't say those things and Tom wasn't the kind of husband who affirmed me enough so that I wouldn't doubt his devotion. I did tell him how much it bothered me that he would stare at her and then act distant towards me whenever she came around, but he wouldn't (*couldn't*) stop the emotional affair.

I felt so lonely, fearful, and sad. I couldn't control or stop his behavior and I truly felt helpless—insane, really—with this vicious cycle. I begged him to respect my wishes and stop paying so much attention to her, but to no avail. It didn't help that he had begun pulling away from me as a result of the shame he felt from his addiction and the fact that he knew he was still participating in it behind my back. His dishonesty was creating anxiety in himself and my inability and refusal to speak truth and stand up for myself was creating craziness in me. I couldn't articulate what was going on in our marriage, but, in my heart, I knew something was wrong.

As we continued attending our church, things got increasingly uncomfortable whenever the other woman was around. Our paths continued to cross and each time I wanted to run away and cry. It was at a Sunday school class social one weekend that I began to reach my "end" at the amount of attention Tom was paying to this lady. I tried to tell Tom how I felt and asked him to be more aware of his actions. He assured me that nothing improper was going on, but the cycle continued and got progressively worse. I believed he was thinking of her and then my mind would start to go crazy over what he might be doing when he was not with me. The feelings inside of me were truly maddening and the conflict inside my soul of wanting to trust my husband wrestled with the "what ifs" in my mind.

The dance continued. I harbored so much anger, hurt, and sadness at his behavior, yet felt shame at myself for being so weak. I honestly thought I was losing my mind. I was continuing in my co-addictive ways by not speaking truth or establishing consistent, firm boundaries that safeguarded my marriage and my own emotional needs. I was also a prisoner to the lie that I wasn't valuable enough to speak up for myself. Like a washing machine, round and round and round we went, never communicating effectively, each one not meeting the other's needs.

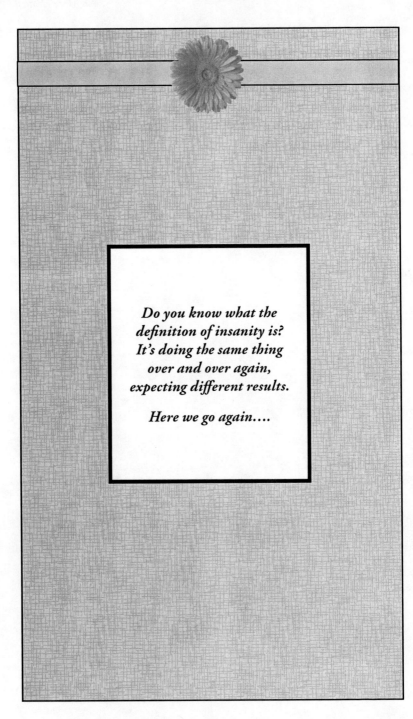

Do you know what the definition of insanity is? It's doing the same thing over and over again, expecting different results.

Here we go again....

10
PACK 'EM UP, MOVE 'EM OUT, INCLUDING ALL HIPPOS, PLEASE!

After an emotional three years with the situation at the church, we left Germany on November 18, 1989, just two weeks before the Berlin Wall came down. Don't get me wrong…we traveled all over Europe and have only good memories of our travels, but the hippos in our lives were starting to multiply and instead of being only two, now we had several. Things were getting crowded and I didn't know what to do with them.

About three months before our tour ended in Europe, our first daughter was born, Elizabeth Hannah. Now things were really getting complicated. I suddenly felt the need to put an extra lock on that closet door and an extra tablecloth on the hippos in our lives, hoping beyond hope that our child wouldn't see them. "If I just kept busy enough and prayed hard enough, well, maybe Tom's problem would magically go away," I thought. The problem with this faulty thinking is this: *No matter where you go, there you are.* And, no matter where we were, whether in Europe or the good ol' United States, our hippos went right along with us. I kept hoping we could leave them behind and start fresh with each military move, but every time the boxes were unpacked, those hippos would reappear.

Next, we moved to Arkansas for Tom's three-month training at the "School House," a C-130 training facility. The C-130 is one of the Air Force's large cargo planes. We lived in a small apartment and it was a happier time in our marriage, as Elizabeth consumed our thoughts and filled our days. She was such a wonderful baby and it seemed for a season that our marriage was going to be better. We didn't speak of the hippos in our lives, but rather chose to focus on our church, Tom's Air Force duties, and raising our daughter. And, you know, for a while, this strategy seemed to work or at least it felt like it was working.

After his training was over, the three of us moved to North Carolina to Pope Air Force base. Tom spent the next three and a half years flying on trips that kept him away more than half the time. We bought our first home, a brand new two-story saltbox style home in a neighborhood that was about twenty-five minutes from the base.

During this time, Tom had "slips" and looked at magazines on some trips. (By the way, what the heck does the term *slip* mean? to trip? to fall? what? That term sounds so lightweight, so fluffy, and so undamaging. In reality, when a husband has an emotional affair and/or a physical affair, let me tell you, "a slip" feels more like a demolition ball ripping through the tender heart of commitment!) Tom's addiction was one that reared its ugly head during times of stress but not on a daily basis. Sometimes he would remain sober for several months. Then, for various reasons, he would falter. Whether it was a month later or a year later, the pain of his behavior was the same.

In spite of my marital turmoil, I had lots of opportunities to sing, giving my life some purpose. I was in the choir at church, sang as a soloist, and led children's choirs while Tom was a Sunday school teacher for a couple's class and a deacon at the medium-sized church we attended. We thrived in this church and loved the area. I know some of you are cringing when you read the words *deacon* and *Sunday school teacher*, but truth be known, our churches are probably full of members who are struggling with pornography issues more than any other addiction. Why? I believe it's because sexual addiction is something that can be easily hidden from those even closest to the addict. It is the "secret" sin, the one that the addict thinks he/she can keep concealed, until it begins to consume their life and wreak havoc.

In August of 1990, Tom got orders that sent him on an eight-month deployment to Kuwait to serve in the Desert Shield/Desert Storm war. Elizabeth was a week shy of being one year old and I remember well the day he left. We lived far from family and I had a small child to raise on my own for an "undisclosed" amount of time. I don't remember feeling much, mostly numb and a lot of fear. It helped knowing that I was one of thousands of wives in the Fayetteville area who were being separated from their husbands for the deployment and that, in a way, brought me comfort. I chose to stay in Fayetteville and "hold down the fort" while he was away. Many of my other friends, however, went home to other states. The 227 days seemed to never end.

What was ironic to me was that during his stay in the tents of Kuwait, affectionately known as "Tent City," Tom remained sober from his addiction to porn. In fact, on one occasion, his tent mate put up a nude poster and Tom asked him to take it down. For eight months, he remained faithful to our marriage vows. When he flew the cargo plane home that day in March of 1991, he walked off the plane a warrior and a victor. He told me of this and I thought, "Finally the problem that has plagued our marriage is gone. This is it. It is over." Somehow in my own naiveté, I breathed a sigh of relief hoping the hippos had donned their turbans or veils, and pitched a tent in the Middle East never to bother us again. Yet, as much as my heart wanted to believe it was *over*, I thought to myself, "That was a little *too* easy."

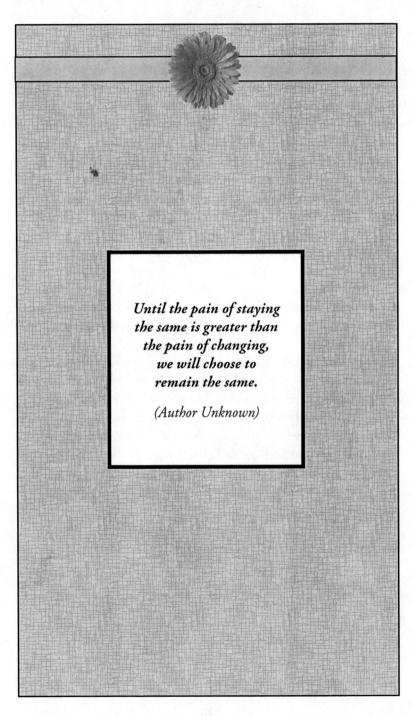

*Until the pain of staying
the same is greater than
the pain of changing,
we will choose to
remain the same.*

(Author Unknown)

11
HIPPO 4

I've got to be honest with you that I am not by nature a patient person. I am the type of person that wants problems fixed and fixed quickly. I don't want to have to rehash things. What's the problem? Okay, here's the band-aid and ointment. Good. Now, let's move on. Well unfortunately, in life, things don't always work that way. I thought the hippos were gone or, rather, my fear-driven belief system hoped they were gone—not because we had been proactive and sought professional help but because, well, because they had gone. Nice little hippos. In my mind, I wanted to believe that they had packed their bags and miraculously left our home sometime between Tom leaving for Desert Shield/Desert Storm and his return in March of 1991. I didn't want to deal with this problem anymore. I was tired of the same old fight and my spirit was weakening. All of this, of course, while neither Tom nor I tried anything new to deal with the issue. It was the same ol' same ol' routine, with the same ol' results: no change.

In November, six months after Tom's return from the war, we found out we were expecting baby number two. (I guess I got over my "tired of the fight" feeling, huh?) When I was about six months pregnant, Tom left on another long trip for two months to do the Bosnia Air Drops in 1992. During his absence, I recorded my first

Gospel album and felt my "career" was taking off. I was singing on the local TV stations, on the radio, and was doing special singing for local churches. Things seemed to be better and I was feeling fulfilled both as a mother, a singer and a wife.

Two months after the Bosnia trip, in July our second beautiful daughter, Alyssa Lauren, was born. In August, Tom was sent to LRAFB (Little Rock Air Force Base) for an eight-week training at the C-130 School House again. While he was away, I kept busy with church activities, friends, playmates for my children, and play dates. It was a lonely time with Tom gone, but I dealt with it. Learning the value of hard work and perseverance by being raised on a farm came in handy. Also, being a mother gave meaning to my life. We had agreed when we got married that he would be the breadwinner of the family and I would raise the children. I really didn't think he was struggling with his addiction and, to be honest, I was so busy with parenting the girls that I didn't even worry about it—another mistake I've learned to regret.

Tom returned home the first part of September after being gone for two long months. We were all so glad to see him and I had missed him terribly. "This is part of being in the military— it requires resiliency, sacrifice, and stamina," I told myself. (yadda, yadda, yadda!) From the moment he walked through the door, though, I could tell something was wrong. After a couple of days of awkwardness, I finally found the courage to confront him. At first, he denied anything was wrong, but after further prodding on my part, he disclosed another fall into temptation. While he had been away during the eight weeks, he had been emotionally and physically unfaithful to me by renting porn videos. He said he had been stressed and needed the release.

I felt an overwhelming rush of disbelief and pain. I thought things were fine. We had two small children and I had asked him to stop and I thought he would, but he didn't…and that was the point. **For the addict, they must want to stop their behaviors in order for change to take place. For the co-dependent, they must want to stop allowing/putting up with the addict's behaviors in order for change to take place.**

See, as a wife of an addict to porn, I can want my husband to choose fidelity and honesty and transparency and intimacy with me all day long, but he has to want those things over the temptation of lust. No amount of crying, begging, or pouting is going to change his behavior. He has to change on his own, not because I've forced him to but because he wants to. This is hard to hear and, oh, so hard to surrender to God, but it's true. I am powerless over his choices and ultimately over his behavior. I am, however, not powerless over my responsibility to speak truth to my husband and tell him my needs.

After this newest disclosure, I screamed, "Get out! I can't live like this anymore!" He began to weep, to sob. Here was this giant of a man reduced to a puddle of tears and shame. He was so entrenched in the disease and sin of sexual addiction that he was truly powerless over its grip on his life. He claimed he "wanted to stop" but didn't know how. For the first time, I could see this stronghold that was literally killing my husband, my marriage, and all the trust I longed to have with this man. Through the tears and sincere sadness of my husband, my heart softened and though my heart felt it would burst from the pain of yet another revelation, I realized that this hippo was not going to go away by merely wishing, wanting, or praying. There was not a tablecloth big enough or fancy enough to cover up the size of it. We were going to need professional help.

The next day, after sleeping in separate bedrooms, we found a Christian counselor and made an appointment. I walked in, sat down, and listened while Tom told our therapist our story. When Tom finished, the therapist looked right at me and said, "He's done quite a number on you, hasn't he?" He went on to explain that I was what therapists would label co-dependent. (Oh, so that's why I had felt crazy for most of our marriage!)

He recommended a book entitled, *Co-dependent No More*, by Melodie Beatty, that I quickly read. It taught me that some personalities, especially those prone to pleasing others, are prime candidates for enabling their husband's or wife's addictions. But it doesn't have to be this way. The book taught me the importance of saying no to other's destructive behaviors (something I wish I had known when I was eighteen). The life-changing principles in the book began equipping me with the ability to lay protective, healthy boundaries and to speak honestly about my own shortcomings. For the first time in my life, I began to speak my mind and to learn how to feel good about making decisions without worrying about what others, including my husband, would think of me. I was taking the first baby steps to becoming free from co-dependent tendencies.

We continued our counseling for a few months and everything in our marriage began to turn around. It was helping, and we both began to practice better communication with each other. We were more honest and, in turn, spoke our needs to each other. Unfortunately, for our marriage, a few months later the Air Force sent Tom to Little Rock on a new assignment. Just when our marriage had found the help it had needed for so long, we were moved to a new place. I really battled feeling angry at God for allowing us to leave when we were finally getting help. We left North Carolina in 1993 and moved to Jacksonville, Arkansas. I remember feeling sad that the counselor who had begun helping us get a handle on our marriage and on our lives was not going to be a part of our lives anymore.

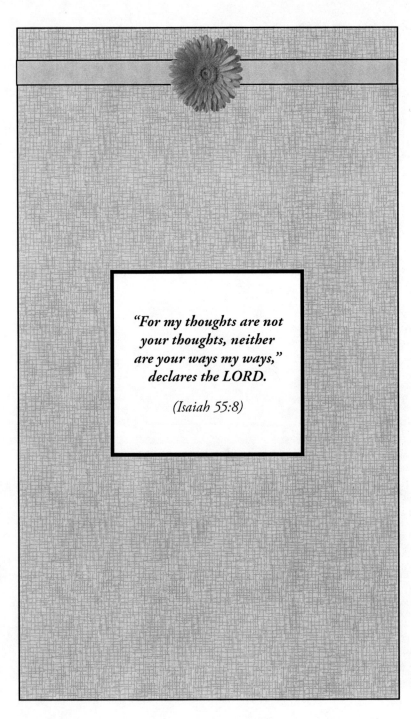

"*For my thoughts are not your thoughts, neither are your ways my ways,*" declares the LORD.

(Isaiah 55:8)

12
NEW ASSIGNMENT, NEW BABY

After leaving North Carolina in 1993, we moved to Jacksonville, Arkansas, home to Little Rock Air Force Base. We bought a home on a beautiful cul-de-sac that bordered a golf course. Our neighbors were wonderful and we immediately found a new church.

It had been less than a year since Tom had made his second major disclosure and since we had gone through counseling. I looked out a new pair of windows and down a new street with the realization that life had changed once again for our family. Sadly, the counselor who had helped us so much in North Carolina was no longer with us and we made the mistake of not immediately finding another one. Again, the addict in Tom and the co-dependent in me thought, "We don't have time for counseling right now…maybe later!" (Dumb! For those of you who feel you and your husband make more mistakes than everyone else, take heart! You are not the only ones and there's hope for you!)

Our talk of "the problem" slowed, and our energies and focus went into resettling. The dust hadn't settled from the move when I told Tom that I felt we shouldn't have any more children. I honestly didn't want to bring another precious child into our family in light of our struggles and in light of the fact that I didn't feel I was adequate as a mom (another lie I believed). Fear of future episodes of infidelity and my pure exhaustion from raising our girls alone while Tom was gone half of each month were evidence for my case. After our discussion, Tom called and made an appointment for "the surgery."

I guess it was about two weeks later that I began feeling nauseous and the thought popped into my mind that maybe I was pregnant. I immediately went to Wal-Mart and got a test. The next morning, first thing, I bolted out of bed and went into our bathroom. I waited anxiously as the indicator went to the plus side. I fell back halfway missing the toilet seat and plopped down in dismay. I couldn't believe it. I was pregnant again! "But God, this can't be in your plan. You know how stressed I am with raising two precious girls, I will surely mess up this third angel if you send me another one. I'm not good at this! Can you reconsider and save this poor little one from all of the mistakes I will undoubtedly make? waah, waah, waah," I cried!

Somehow in the ramblings of my pleading with God, his still small voice spoke to my heart and said, "Fear not, my child. I know full well what is best for you." I wish I could say I felt totally confident from that moment on, but I didn't. I did, however, take a deep breath, and, with my hands in the air, I surrendered to his plans for me and for our family.

In August of the next year, Victoria Anne was added to our family. I remember the joy and sheer panic that simultaneously flooded my heart when I would think about the incredible responsibility of raising three small children. It was all so overwhelming. Then I would look at her beautiful face and into the faces of our other two angels and feel the guilt and pressure of wanting to parent to perfection. I could not let them down, because they were so wonderful. That, of course, was my addiction to perfectionism and performance that ran parallel to Tom's addiction to porn. I falsely believed that I had to do things well in order to find my own validation and acceptance from others, and Tom wanted to find his worth and acceptance as a man, even if it was from air-brushed women in magazines and videos.

After giving birth to Victoria, I went through post-partum depression. It was one of the darkest and scariest times of my life. Tom was gone a lot with his job again, but the secure, confident person I had been during my high school years was suddenly replaced with a terrified, insecure child. I awoke every morning to a panic attack. At the very realization that I was awake, my throat would close, I would gasp for air, and a feeling of absolute horror would grip me. The overwhelming reality that I was responsible for three little lives was too great for my mind to comprehend.

I called my parents many times in the wee hours of those frantic mornings, longing to hear some voices of sanity that could give me some sense of stability in the house of cards that my emotions had become. I remember reaching for Tom when he was home and clinging to him like a terrified child. I was utterly scared to death. I couldn't get a grip, no matter how much I willed my mind—nothing worked.

It was at this time that Tom began working on his master's degree. Not only was he gone during his normal work week teaching at the School House, now he was gone two nights a week. Unlike the normal TDY's (temporary duty, trips), because he was an instructor on the C-130 at the School House, he was working a normal five day work week for the most part. He was gone most days and then for class and when he was home, he was studying. It was a huge sacrifice for everyone, but I really supported him and wanted him to succeed. It took him two years to complete it and when he was done, we were all so glad!

It was during this stressful time, that I began to have panic attacks almost every day. Thankfully, I had the courage and enough self love to go and see a psychologist who immediately prescribed some anti-depressants. She smiled after listening to my story and said, "Kolinda, you're not crazy! You are just completely overwhelmed with the demands of your life. You are raising three small children, virtually alone, so the help you need is not there. I think if you will just take this prescription and find a way to relax each day, you will make it through this."

So, I took a low-dose anti-depressant and stumbled through the next six months, only to find I wasn't much better. I would drive past a cemetery on my way home from the grocery store and start gasping for air. "Oh, my God! I'm going to die!" I would think. "I can't die! Too many little people depend on me." I truly felt like I was cast in a horror movie as the leading actress. Only problem was, I couldn't get out of this scene. I couldn't turn off the cameras and walk off the set. I was stuck in a situation that was forcing me down on my knees to utter dependence on God.

God was using this time of trial to teach me something about himself. In Isaiah 43:19 it says, "See, I am doing a new thing! Now it springs up; do you not perceive it? I am making a way in the desert and streams in the wasteland." I am making a way in the *desert* and streams in the *wasteland*. My soul felt about as parched as any desert sojourner could feel. It was like I was a prickly cactus in a hot, hellish desert and my emotional stability was like a vanishing mirage. I no longer felt secure in who I was. God, who is faithful, though, began to teach me about dependence on him. He began to show me the abundance of his sufficiency and how empty all of my past accomplishments were in comparison to his eternal greatness and sufficiency.

This wisdom didn't come to me in a way I would have anticipated. God began to reveal himself to me in still, small ways. I began to learn to commit my day to him and to surrender to his will. As soon as I awoke, I would seek him and call to him in prayer, asking for help to *trust him* to order my day. I began prioritizing, spending quality time reading my Bible and believing his promises. I didn't always see the results I wanted, but I continued no matter how tired and worn out I felt from the day's demands. Instead of talking on the phone or cleaning the house when the girls took their nap, I would pray or meditate on the Word. It became *life* to me. And if I was feeling tired, I allowed myself the right to take a nap when the girls did, listening to my physical needs and nurturing them. I learned the value of self-care and of self-respect.

God taught me the process of sanctification, of renewing my mind, and of stepping out in faith when all around me at times was lonely, scary, or dark. My faith suddenly turned from insecurity to strength because my foundation changed from reliance on self and others, especially on Tom, to reliance on a power that is big enough to provide all that I needed. God was allowing me to walk through this storm in order to teach me to rely on him, because he knew about the struggles in the road ahead. He knew I needed to know how to rely on him fully and to completely trust his sufficiency in my life, not resting on my husband or any other man to meet my needs.

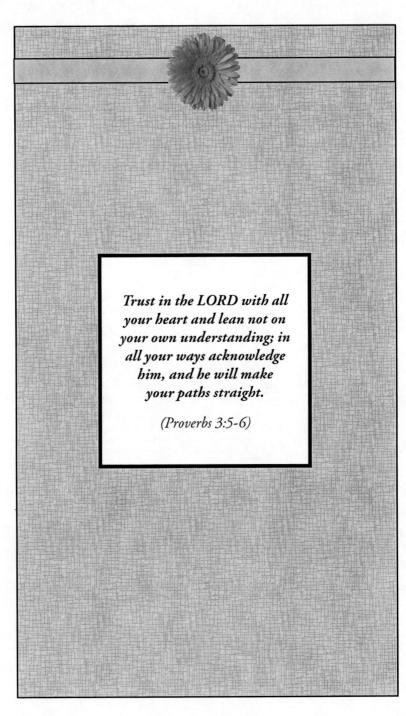

Trust in the LORD with all your heart and lean not on your own understanding; in all your ways acknowledge him, and he will make your paths straight.

(Proverbs 3:5-6)

13
COMMERCIAL AIRLINES

In July of 1996, we left Arkansas and the military life we had known for eleven years. The hopes we had had of Tom getting his master's degree and being promoted to major were for loss and we had to make the hard decision of staying in the Air Force with no promotion indefinitely or getting out. This was a hard decision for both of us as we had loved the military experience and the many friends we had made over the years. So, after much prayer, we opted to leave the Air Force and Tom began the grueling process of looking for employment in the "outside" world. After several interviews, he was hired with Northwest Airlines and we were ecstatic. While we were in between jobs and awaiting Tom's training with Northwest, we spent three weeks in Illinois with my parents, who had graciously invited us to stay with them.

With a new job for Tom, new move, new environment, and much change in our lives, I was feeling the stress. I wasn't sure why, but I started having panic attacks again. It seemed that any time I was faced with more stress, my emotions would falter. I was not consistent in my self-care. It felt like *work* for me to take care of myself as I tried to balance caring for everyone else in my life. I longed for stability. All during this time, I felt estranged from Tom—disconnected, alone. I couldn't put a finger on why I felt this way, but I knew in my heart (my gut) that something was wrong again.

I knew that Tom was still looking at pornography, but I didn't want to face the reality that he was not willing to change or to confront his addiction. In my denial, I chose to overlook it, because the pain of facing the reality of lost dreams and betrayal by the one I loved was too great to bear. Denial is such a deceptive and false way to cope with life. At times, it has kept me from asking the hard questions and facing the giants in my life. Instead of being the mature, godly woman I was created to be, my denial has imprisoned me in fear and insecurity. It has also been the greatest deterrent for Satan to keep me from living an abundant life. Making excuses and denying what is right in front of us never does anybody any good. It takes courage to stand up against the hippos in our lives and to find answers and that was one character quality I was lacking.

I could list a hundred different reasons for not taking care of myself and for not confronting Tom for his infidelity to me and to our marriage vows. I could blame and make a great case for why he needed to change, but the truth is he didn't want to change. He was elusive, dishonest, deceptive, and, literally, unwilling to seek help for his addiction that he knew was raging out of control. I was immature, driven by fear, dishonest not only with Tom but also with myself about my pent up emotions; I was angry as hell that I had to raise our girls mostly alone. In reality, my methods of coping with life were just as unhealthy as Tom's. We were just getting by and this reality brought me more unhappiness than I wanted to admit. I longed for an intimacy with Tom that the biblical Song of Songs speaks of and, in my little girl heart, I still dreamed it could be a reality.

*Remember the former things,
those of long ago; I am God,
and there is no other;
I am God, and there is none like
me. I make known the end from the
beginning, from ancient times, what
is still to come. I say: My purpose will
stand, and I will do all that I please.
Listen to me, you stubborn-hearted,
you who are far from righteousness.
I am bringing my righteousness
near, it is not far away; and my
salvation will not be delayed.*

(Isaiah 46:9-10, 12-13a)

14
MINNESOTA

For more than ten years, I had worked hard at denying and hiding that Tom was addicted to pornography. Though I knew Tom knew I hated him looking at it, I didn't lay any firm boundaries with him, stating my needs. He, in turn, kept quiet and figured if I didn't ask him about it, there really wasn't a need to tell me. It was a silent agreement we had made. My parents didn't know, his parents and family didn't know, my closest friends didn't know, and, most of all, my church family didn't know. Heck, I didn't know for sure, because I chose to tuck the hippos nicely away in the closets of every house we had ever owned.

At the core of my decision to hide the truth, was my pride and a deep-seated fear of rejection. "*If* they knew, they wouldn't understand. *If* they knew, they would reject both Tom and me, as if we had the plague," I told myself. "I mean, a deacon and a worship leader having such horrible, sinful problems in their marriage. Aren't Christian leaders supposed to have it all together? For shame, for shame." And, that's exactly what I felt...shame. The funny thing, though, was Tom was feeling the exact same thing, yet neither one of us was able to talk about our feelings to each other or to anyone we knew.

After moving to Minnesota, we found a good church that we began attending in the Minneapolis area. Tom and I became members of a small group that met locally on Sunday nights. At first, I was hesitant to connect with the others. I was suffering from depression both from living a lie in my married life and from the lack of sunlight for which Minnesota is known. As we continued to attend the weekly meetings, the members would tell us how much we meant to them. In time, I began to let my guard down and risked trusting again. I honestly longed for a group of Christians who would walk with us through this fire and be willing to stay the course, loving us unconditionally.

I made friends with one of the wives in the group whose daughter played with one of ours. We saw each other during the week, and I slowly began to feel like this was someone I could trust. After several months though, I noticed she was making comments to me about Tom. Things like, "I can tell Tom works out. He looks like he takes really good care of himself," and "Tom's the kind of man who's going to age gracefully and distinctively like Sean Connery." I tried to dismiss the comments as nothing, but my sixth sense began to wave the red flag.

A few months later, we attended a special Christmas social at one of the couple's homes. It was a festive evening and everyone was dressed up. I felt especially "pretty" that evening—you know the kind of pretty when your hair is cooperating, your clothes are looser than normal, and your skin has neither a pimple nor a wrinkle showing—that kind of pretty! As we mingled with the other couples, I noticed Tom staring and glancing repeatedly at my friend. Instantly, I remembered the times before when he had had emotional affairs with those other women. "Not again," I thought.

I felt uneasy. Tom and I had been playing the "Hide the Hippo" game for so many years that upon seeing his glances at that other woman, I knew I didn't *know* my husband and I certainly didn't trust him. I knew that I had not established any firm boundaries with him, setting limits to what I would and would not put up with in our marriage. I was too busy raising the girls, after all, and used that as my excuse for not "showing up" and speaking my truth. These unhealthy ways of living only perpetuated my insecurities.

After we got home from the party that night, we started getting ready for bed. I was upset, but did my usual "stuffing" of my feelings and didn't dare tell him how I really felt. I passively and aggressively ignored him, sulking off into the bathroom, getting dressed behind closed doors, putting on my Laura Ingalls' flannel pajamas, making sure he got the message!

Wives, one word of advice to you: Men don't "get the message" unless you speak the audible words and perhaps even draw them a picture! So, if you think that huffing and puffing and not saying a word to him will make him magically understand your deepest longings and feelings, forget it! You must speak your truth and needs, clearly!

Tom, on the other hand, got a brilliant idea to be more open with me about his thought life. Now, where that idea came from, I am not really sure (Hades, perhaps?), but he thought it would be a good idea to share. So, he began, "Honey, I want to be more open with you about some of the thoughts I've been having. I noticed 'Angie' tonight at the party and was noticing how pretty she looked." See, in his male mind, he believed that by being honest with his thoughts that would somehow be beneficial to our relationship and would open the lines of communication.

As his words hit my ears and then sunk down to my heart, I remember feeling about as low as I could feel. He hadn't told me I looked pretty that night. I felt my blood begin to boil. All the years of resentment about his addiction and affairs of the heart came to the surface. I began to verbally unload. I honestly wanted him to feel all the pain I had been stuffing for so many years. You see, whenever people fight, it's hardly ever because of what has just happened. Nine times out of ten, the straw that breaks the camel's back is merely at the top of a haystack of unmet needs, unresolved feelings, and violated boundaries. Instead of being honest with Tom about my feelings and setting boundaries over the course of our marriage, I had a mile-high pile of resentment toward him, and I began firing one bullet after another at him.

I wish I could say that our conversation that night ended with me setting boundaries while both of us shared our deepest feelings and concerns, talking in a civilized manner. I cannot, however. We went to bed angry, confused, and more resentful toward each other than we had been before the night began. Neither one of us were equipped with the know-how of good, healthy communication. We longed for it but didn't have the skills.

The next morning, Tom announced to me that he didn't want to attend the small group anymore because of the situation with the other woman's comments and his actions the night before. I agreed. We stopped going and instead of speaking to the other woman about her inappropriate comments and later finding help with our huge marital struggles, we put another tablecloth over our hippopotamus in the living room. By running from our "stuff," it only prolonged the inevitable.

You see, the trouble with running from our "hippos" is that they don't go away. We are designed for healthy, meaningful relationships and when they are out of kilter and unhealthy, God will align them in such a way that we have to face them! He will pursue us, because he loves us that much and wants us to live in harmony with others, speaking truth and working things out. It may be a day, a week, or even years, but God will not allow us to keep on running from our stuff, especially if we are his child in the faith.

A few months later, I ran into "Angie," and she inquired about why we weren't coming to small group anymore. I made up some excuse about our busy lives. I remember feeling frustrated that I hadn't been honest due to my fear of confrontation when all the while my dishonesty was only making things worse. God wasn't done with this situation and he wasn't about to let me leave Minnesota without making me face the music and deal.

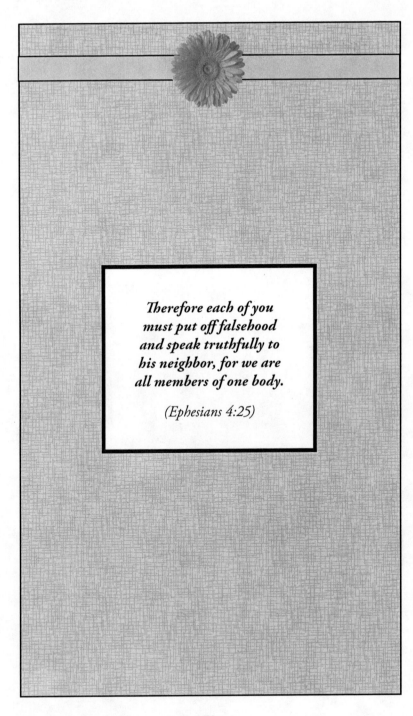

Therefore each of you
must put off falsehood
and speak truthfully to
his neighbor, for we are
all members of one body.

(Ephesians 4:25)

15
SPEAKING THE TRUTH – FINALLY!

I t was during this most emotional time in our lives that a miracle occurred. One day, Tom called me into our front living room and told me he wanted to talk to me about something. As the conversation ensued, he began to tell me that he had been praying and felt like maybe our family needed to take a step of faith and move. My eyes widened and my heart was curious as to where this move might be. He went on to say that he thought we should move to the low-income area of downtown Minneapolis and live as our church's staff did, trying to live out our faith helping those less fortunate.

I think my eyes opened as big as saucers at this point because I remember thinking, "He's got to be kidding! Move to the *inner* city? I'm a country girl. I **hate** crowded, bustling cities and would never want to *live* there? No way! Let alone, raise our girls there!" Of course, I was not shy about my intense feelings and shared them passionately.

He swallowed hard and said, "Well, I thought you might say something like that, so I had another thought about where we should move. I think we should move to Nashville, Tennessee, and see if God has something there for you in the Christian music industry." Like the moment when Tom proposed, I was frozen and don't recall being able to answer for a few seconds. Nashville? My dream place to live, the place I had longed to be for so many years. Would I like to live there? You betcha!

In January of 2001, we began the task of preparing our Minnesota home for the move southward to Tennessee. We were very busy with the myriad of details that moving requires and so I thought the issue with the woman from the small group was moot.

I was walking out of the front doors of the elementary school one morning as "Angie" was entering. I remember feeling a sense of dread at seeing her. All the feelings of resentment toward her comments about Tom flooded my emotions. We stopped and made small talk and then as I was leaving she said, "Oh, tell Tom I said hello and give him a hug!" I couldn't believe it! I hadn't seen this woman for several months and then when I did run into her she didn't want to talk to me, she wanted to talk about my husband! (I let the door swing shut but had the thick glass door not separated us, I would have body slammed her to the earth, hoping small pieces of rock and dirt would embed themselves in her flirtatious mouth. Okay, I'm exaggerating, but I couldn't believe her boldness!)

I went home that day and shared with Tom all that had happened. He then went on to tell me that he thought I should talk to her about her comments. He thought that honesty would be the best policy—imagine that. So, I prayed and prayed about what to do.

It was at this same time that I was also meeting with another lady from the small group each week for a Bible study. We began to pray together about the problem, seeking the LORD's help and direction. Because I wanted to seek the counsel of my friends, I told two of the other ladies in the group. One of them just laughed and told me not to worry about it. The other friend and I prayed for weeks, trying to find an answer to our question. To be honest, the last thing I wanted to do before moving was to get into a confrontation with someone.

After some time, both Tom and my Bible study friend agreed that it would be best to go to her and share my feelings about her comments. I really struggled with this because I *HATED* confrontation and had absolutely no desire to start something with this woman because I knew we were leaving. My goal in sharing our story with her was to tell her about Tom's addiction so that maybe she would understand *why* her comments bothered me and *why* they were so damaging. By being honest with someone from church, I was hopeful that I could finally confront the hippos in our lives and face them, instead of trying so desperately to hide them.

I found the courage to call her and asked if I could come over and talk with her about some things. She agreed and we set up a time for me to do so. I walked into her small kitchen and felt such uneasiness in the pit of my stomach, because I knew I would be confronting her about her actions, and because I was risking being honest about Tom's addiction.

I began our conversation by trying to let her know that I was not blaming her or falsely accusing her. Then, I took a deep breath and told her about our "hippopotamus." I told her of Tom's lifelong struggle to break free from the stronghold of pornography and how much our marital trust had been broken because of his improprieties. Because of this, her comments had bothered me, greatly. I wanted her to know so that our friendship could be saved and we could move on. She claimed to be a godly woman and I also wanted to make her aware of how her comments about Tom truly didn't line up with the person she claimed to be.

After I finished, her eyes filled with tears. She apologized for what she had said and claimed that her intentions were not to be flirtatious. She was noticeably shaken, as was I for I knew the cat was out of the bag and she would have the ability to either crucify Tom and me with her newfound knowledge or walk with us in spite of it. We both cried and then hugged and then laughed together. I felt so relieved that I had mustered up the courage to speak to my friend and to let her into my world. I was hopeful that a new door had opened for me in being more honest with others.

I went home and told Tom about our conversation. He was glad and we both felt that maybe we had finally found a group of friends who would dare to walk alongside us through the nightmare of sexual addiction. We knew that even though we would soon be in another state, that if they would dare to understand our situation, we would have friends praying for us and standing with us no matter what the distance was between us. Our feeling of elation lasted about a day. The next afternoon, I went to check my emails; I received one from her. Instead of the words of friendship I had anticipated, she wrote a blasting note retracting everything from the previous day's conversation and accusing me of falsely blaming her. I wanted to die. "So much for being honest with fellow church members," I thought.

It took me two whole days to muster up the courage again to call her on the phone in hopes that this raging inferno could somehow be extinguished. I left a message and she called me back later that night. I shook as we talked. The conversation at first was very tense and I could hear the resentment in her voice and the judgment in her words. We trudged through our initial conversation and finally reached a place of calm and rational communicating. As we talked, the ice began to melt and the walls began to crumble. I told her how very much her friendship meant to me and how I wanted to keep in touch. By the end of the conversation, we were both laughing and I honestly felt like everything was mended and healthy. The last words I told her were to keep in touch and she agreed. I hung up the phone and felt a load of relief, thinking that I had finally found the courage to confront my issues and to not run from my feelings. I had been *honest* with her and things had worked out.

Tom and I continued working out the details of our move over the next few months. It was a busy, busy time and all of our energies were focused on one thing: getting to Tennessee. One day, I got a call from one of the women from the small group; they wanted to throw me a farewell party. I remember feeling uncomfortable at their request, as we hadn't attended the small group for more than six months.

At the party, I saw "Angie" and she was very distant and cold. "I hope she hasn't gone back on her word again. She sure is acting funny," I thought. As I left the party that night, I saw her talking to another woman in the group. I said a big "goodbye" and everyone else looked up and smiled and said their farewells. She, on the other hand, just kept on talking, making an obvious effort to ignore me. In the pit of my stomach, I knew something was wrong, but thought,

"Well, hopefully, she will be honest and let me know if she's thinking something different than what she told me in our last conversation." With the hope of moving to Tennessee and starting fresh, I dusted off my shoes and waved goodbye that night to the women of that group knowing full well that things were not as good with "Angie" as they had seemed.

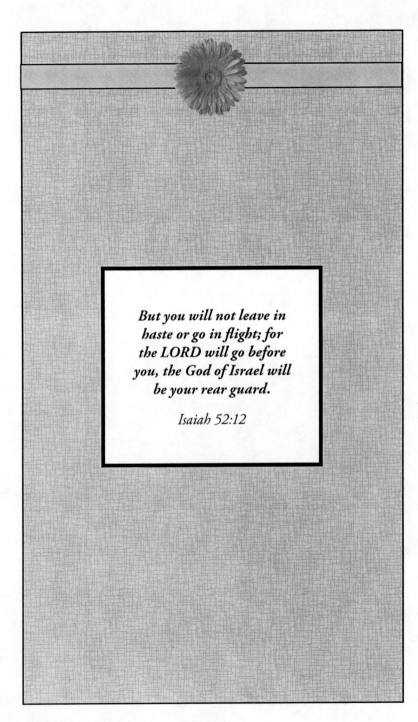

> *But you will not leave in haste or go in flight; for the LORD will go before you, the God of Israel will be your rear guard.*
>
> *Isaiah 52:12*

16
THE PROMISED LAND

The next few weeks were a blur. We purged, packed, sold our house, and worked toward closing on a hobby farm we had purchased in Tennessee. It was the end of May and we had a goal of closing on the house in Minnesota by June 7, packing the last of our belongings, and beginning the trek to Tennessee on June 8. I felt overwhelmed, yet overjoyed knowing that we were moving out of the "tundra" and on to a new life and to a warmer climate. I mistakenly thought that if we could just move down south, my marriage would be better and that the communication problems Tom and I had would somehow vanish into the warm, thin air.

With the help of my dear parents, our closest friends, and some dear neighbors, we left Minnesota on June 8, 2001. These people were the salt of the earth to us, an example of "Jesus with skin on." Tom and I knew that we were supposed to move to Tennessee. We thought it was for me to pursue my music/voice degree at Belmont University. Little did we know that God had other plans for us that far surpassed our wildest dreams. The funny thing with God, though, is that his ways are *not* our ways and his plans are definitely not anything we could conjure up in our finite minds (Isaiah 55:8).

As we turned onto our lane and started driving down the hill, our oldest daughter, Elizabeth, then only nine years old, stuck her head out of the window and yelled, "We're home! We're home!" We all laughed and cried and felt such a sense of relief in knowing that God had brought us to Tennessee for some wonderful reason.

The girls ran through the empty house, squealing and checking out all the new secret places. The house had been empty for over 8 months and we found a boatload of spiders and bugs that we had to quickly expel. The pool in the back yard was brimming with green, slimy algae. There was work to be done, but our spirits ran high and nothing seemed too great or too daunting. It all felt so new and exciting and so hopeful.

We settled into our new home and began to do the normal things families do when they are in a new area. The girls attended the public schools that were close to our home and I spent the first weeks unpacking boxes, greeting the neighbors and becoming familiar with our new surroundings.

We passed a small country church each day called Hillview Baptist Church. The very first weekend we were in Tennessee, the girls and I attended that Sunday. As we walked in the front door, a tall friendly man greeted us. We immediately felt the love of Christ from every member in the church, and we were hooked! We became instant friends and began serving where they needed us. It felt like home in the way that watching *The Andy Griffith Show* makes you feel. And, we truly were – home.

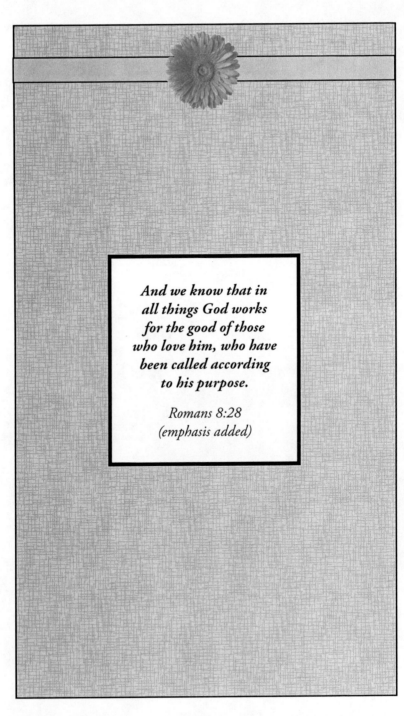

And we know that in all things God works for the good of those who love him, who have been called according to his purpose.

Romans 8:28
(emphasis added)

17

AFTERMATH

Two months had passed since we pulled out of the short driveway in the carbon copy neighborhood we had left in Minnesota. Most of the boxes were unpacked and for the most part, our new life in Tennessee was feeling very much "at peace." I remember the day well. I went to get the mail and found an envelope with a Minnesota address on it. I recognized the name of one of the members in the small group as the lady who had thrown the farewell party for me earlier in May. I remember thinking how nice it was to be getting a card from her. The letter looked like a small Hallmark card you might anticipate opening from a dear friend or loved one. As I opened it though and began to read, I felt a sense of dread, of immense sadness come over me. The woman, a close friend of "Angie's" began a long discourse making small talk about the girls and how did we like Tennessee, and so on.

As I scanned down the pages I read the words, "Satan's minion" and my heart sank. I read quickly, my heart racing as I read the harsh words. I immediately felt a sense of fear that "Angie" had changed her mind and had gone back on her parting words to me of owning her part of the incident with Tom. I wondered with dread at what had transpired in my absence. As I read the letter, it spoke of how "Angie" had told her that I had accused her of having feelings towards Tom and that my comments were completely out of line. Then, she went on to say that the small group of women had taken it upon themselves to call a special meeting to discuss the situation with their husbands present to discuss what had happened between "Angie" and me. I remember feeling sick to my stomach, first because I was no longer living in Minnesota where I could defend myself and second because this letter was beginning to sound like a witch hunt and I was being called the "witch!"

The letter informed me of my wrongdoing, never once mentioning the fact I had been honest with "Angie" about Tom's addiction. The letter went on to accuse me of being Satan's assistant, one of his minions. I couldn't believe it. I had risked being honest about Tom's addiction, about WHY "Angie's" comments bothered me and then she had turned it all around, bringing shame to our name. Here was her friend accusing me of doing Satan's work.

I trembled and cried as I read the words of that letter. I took it to Tom and together, we wept. Tom asked me not to respond to the note. He wanted to write to the men who had been pulled into the mess and explain to them his side of the story. He hoped to enlighten these "brothers in Christ," and share the *truth* of his addiction in hopes they would at the very least understand why I had confronted "Angie" about her remarks.

Tom wrote that letter to the men of the small group. For the first time, he openly shared his struggles with pornography, his fight to become free and how the addiction had been a silent killer of our marriage for over 15 years. He was completely transparent with them. After he wrote it, I remember feeling such anger at the way I was being treated, fear at what the outcome of his letter might be and yet such gladness that he was being honest after so many years.

I wrote a letter of apology to the women in the group for any harm I had done by not going to "Angie" right away. I did try calling "Angie" in hopes that we could talk, but she never returned my calls. Three weeks later, I received another note from the same lady who had sent the first, with no mention of anything of substance, only niceties about the weather and such. Another one of the ladies from the group called and we tried to talk things out but the damage had been done. (Both my letter and Tom's disclosure letter to the men were written more than 8 years ago at the writing of this book. No one else from that small group has ever responded to either one of our letters.)

Though I tried to speak my truth in love to "Angie" it seemed at first my efforts had backfired. Yet, somehow in the middle of the pain I felt from the way it all turned out, God began to show me that He was working in this situation and that His plans for us would be for the good. Even though the initial outcome from trying to be transparent seemed to fail, God wasn't done with us yet....

"Something inside of me finally was in a place of complete surrender, my body in a broken heap, submitted, done. I had hit the bottom of trying to pretend everything was 'okay,' 'fine,' 'good.' I was finally ready to take the tablecloth off the hippos in our life and face the truth of Tom's addiction."

Kolinda King Duer

18

A New Beginning

God promises to finish the work He starts in each of us who are called by His name. At the time we were walking through the fire with the situation from Minnesota, we had no idea what God was ultimately trying to do in our lives. Feeling rejected by the small group was hurtful and something neither one of us would want to walk through again. But God is faithful and He used that incident to begin the long awaited process of healing Tom of his addiction to porn and me of my co-dependency.

It was a Friday night sometime in June of 2004. We had been living in Tennessee for about three years and life was good in all other respects. We were enjoying the beautiful weather that middle Tennessee is known for and had started to meet some wonderful people and make some amazing friends. I was busy doing maternal things, involved with the girls and their activities. Tom had returned from a week long trip and was to be home for a few days. I remember I was in the kitchen cooking supper when he came in and stood by the refrigerator. I looked up only to see that all too familiar look on his face. I asked him what was wrong and he went on to tell me that he had had another "slip up" with his problem.

For the first time in the seventeen years of our marriage, something snapped inside of me. Suddenly it was different from all of the other times of Tom's indiscretions and my enabling. I suddenly felt bold and strong inside and went on to tell him that I couldn't, no I **wouldn't**, live like this anymore. I told him I was done, really done this time and that I wanted him out.

Of course, the usual performance incurred, with his apology and his promise to do better, but this time I didn't waiver. I chose instead to tell him, "*No More.*" Inside, I felt like I had to do something drastic, something new and take a stand against this demon of pornography that had so ravaged my life, my husband's life and, most of all, my marriage. The girls were getting older and I finally realized this Hippo had to go once and for all. I couldn't forgive and forget anymore and I wanted Tom to know that the game was over. The dance was over and most of all, I decided the enabling of his addiction that I had been doing was over. I was not going to participate any more.

I didn't know how, I didn't know where and I didn't know when, but somehow I knew I had to reach through my deep insecurities and grab hold of God's truth that He had a plan for us, one that would ultimately bring us to a place of glorifying Him. I suddenly knew, though, that the only way for that plan to come to fruition would be if some drastic changes were made in our marriage. Something inside of me finally was in a place of complete surrender, my body in a broken heap, submitted, done. I had hit the bottom of trying to pretend everything was "okay," "fine," "good." I wasn't willing to put any more tablecloths over any more hippos. I wasn't willing to play like we were Ward and June Cleaver anymore. I was finally ready to take the tablecloth off the hippos in our life and face the truth of Tom's addiction.

The next morning, I got up and found Tom in the office. He had been up earlier and had been on the phone making an appointment with a therapist in the Nashville area who specializes in sexual addiction recovery. He went in to see her that next day. For the first time in our seventeen years of marriage, I saw Tom doing something proactive about his problem by making an appointment on his own. I decided to give him a chance to see if he was sincere about changing. I watched Tom take his first steps toward seeking sobriety for himself. I waited to see if he meant it. As I watched and waited, I was cautiously hopeful while being intentional about my own self-care and listening to my heart's needs. No sex until we both got some professional help of some type, lots of space and cautious listening were three boundaries I placed in our marriage. Tom respected my wishes and in the deepest places of my wounded heart, I began to see a glimmer of hope and healing.

Tom began seeing the therapist on a regular basis and then attended an intensive workshop called Bethesda Workshops for addicts the following fall. It was a five-day intensive session that used clinically proven therapy for addicts (both men and women). When we picked him up that Sunday morning, he seemed very drained, tired and it was obvious that the event was exhausting. He didn't say much about it for the first day. Then he told me about the life-changing experience, trying to capture in words the essence of it.

For weeks after this, he continued seeing the therapist until he became active in Sexaholics Anonymous and Alcoholics Anonymous. Both organizations are renowned for the Twelve Steps that are the cornerstone of their success. I began to see a difference in him that was truly noticeable. Hope started to seep into the tiny crevices of our home shining light into the dark places. It was a new beginning.

Part 2: What I've Learned

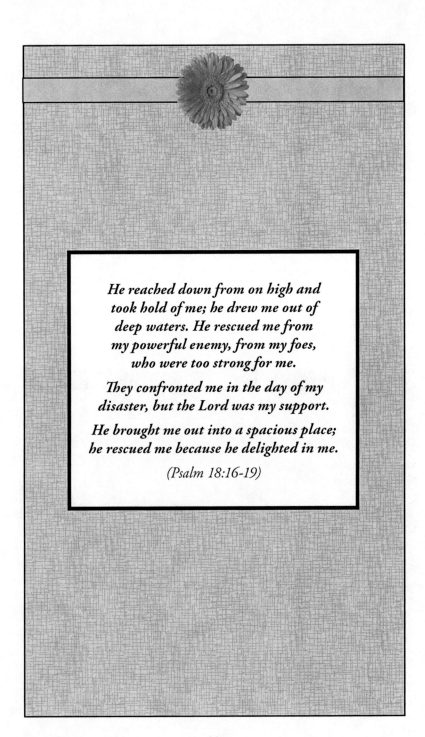

He reached down from on high and took hold of me; he drew me out of deep waters. He rescued me from my powerful enemy, from my foes, who were too strong for me.

They confronted me in the day of my disaster, but the Lord was my support.

He brought me out into a spacious place; he rescued me because he delighted in me.

(Psalm 18:16-19)

WHAT I'VE LEARNED

One of the goals I had when I began writing this memoir was to unashamedly share my story and to offer some practical solutions to the issue of pornography addiction. The first half of the book chronicles the relevant experiences I had that led up to our move from the "Tundra" of Minnesota to the "Promised Land" of Tennessee, from the point in my life when all of my coping mechanisms that had once worked for me suddenly weren't working anymore.

After arriving in our new state in June of 2001, I felt so much hope for our lives. As you will read, though, God used some unexpected trials to spur us onto a journey of healing. It was from those circumstances that God began to mold and shape us into His plans for us. One of my favorite quotes is from Dr. Leslie Parrott. She says, "Until we are willing to do the hard work of becoming whole on our own, all of our relationships will fall disappointingly flat." God has taught me just how important it is to do that hard work of becoming whole as a person in my spiritual, emotional and physical realms.

The following chapters are just that: glimpses of God's grace in my life and His lessons of love to both Tom and me. At the end of each one, there is a ● "Facing the Hippo" challenge to you to take what you have learned and apply it. I pray that as you read each one, you will find the courage you need to do so and along the way, be transformed and unashamedly ready to face your own hippos!

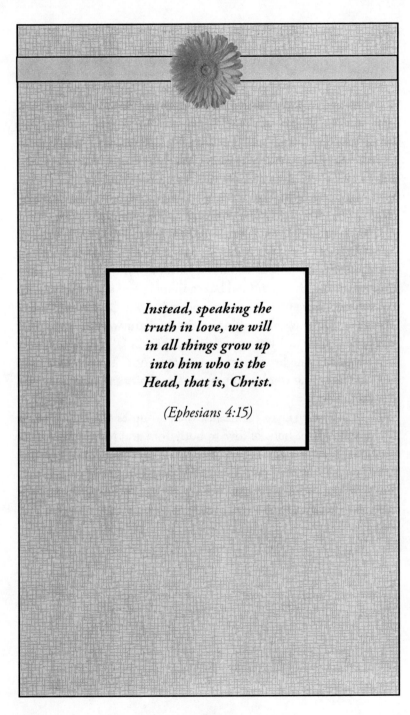

Instead, speaking the truth in love, we will in all things grow up into him who is the Head, that is, Christ.

(Ephesians 4:15)

19
NO MORE HIPPOS!!

As I witnessed Tom's sobriety and saw his obvious efforts to change, I was motivated to look inside myself and do some long overdo self-care. I started seeing Tom's therapist and went as often as I could. During one of our sessions, the counselor said something to me that pierced my heart. She advised both Tom and me to tell our daughters about the addiction problem and to be "real" with them.

Immediately, I didn't feel good about this. After all, I had spent the last fourteen years trying to hide the reality of their daddy's addiction. To tell them seemed counter to all of my desperate efforts. She mentioned the fact that we had a "hippopotamus" in our living room and everyone in the house saw it, *including the girls*, but no one wanted to address its presence. She spoke the truth that the girls knew something was wrong; they just didn't know *what* was wrong. To be honest with them would deflate the power of the hippo and would actually create an openness that would open the floodgates to our family's healing.

We went home that day and I had to pray! I thought, "Lord, I've tried so hard to protect my children from this reality in our lives. How can it be in *your* will that we tell them what is going on in our marriage? How can this help?" I did not want to do anything to hurt the wonderful father/daughter relationship that Tom had built with them. After praying, I didn't get a lightning bolt answer sprawled across the sky. I did, however, feel certain that God wanted Tom and me to begin the long journey of recovery from sexual addiction and codependency and the first place to begin that healing would be at home. God also began revealing to me the truth that sexual addiction is shrouded in shame and holds its captives in bondage. The only way to break free of the stronghold is to face it with courage and truth.

After about a week's worth of fervent prayer, a peace permeated both our hearts. We went to each girl's room and spoke to them about the hippo in our home. Each daughter needed to know only what was necessary to understand the situation. To tell every graphic detail would have been detrimental to their spiritual and emotional well being. For each daughter, I had prayed that Tom would know how much to say to them, while being sensitive to the Holy Spirit's leading. I stood by Tom and he did the talking. For our fifteen year old, he told her that he had a problem with pornography and that he had looked at inappropriate pictures on the Internet and in magazines and videos. He went on to share how much this had hurt me and that what he had done was very wrong. He also told her that he had sinned against God and that he had asked for forgiveness both from God and from me. For our twelve year old, he shared a similar story and answered only questions that she asked, making sure not to be too graphic. For our ten year old, he shared that he had looked at pictures of other women and that what he had done had hurt me.

I was amazed at how each of our girls handled the news. I knew they did not fully understand the full extent of the addiction and that was okay. Just knowing we had given them the gift of knowing about the "hippopotamus" was freeing. It somehow opened the door to future conversations while empowering them to feel safe to talk to us about *anything*. I believe this humbling of both Tom and me to share our "stuff" was the beginning of our family's healing.

Facing Your Hippos This Week:

If you and your husband are seeking professional help and are in agreement to talk to your children in truth, I want to encourage you to do so. Speak to your counselor and seek their advice before you speak to your children. Pray. Then, when you feel it is in God's timing, sit each child down, and in their *age-appropriate levels*, speak your truth.

The beauty of this exercise is that even though it is hard to do, the courage and integrity of speaking truth to your children is an incredible example of godly wisdom and trust in God's provision and strength. Our kids learn more from our example, from our humility, and from our obedience than they do from any sermon. Remember: when you choose to speak the truth and face the hippo, you are fighting against strongholds and making a new way for your children to live and grow spiritually. It is breaking generational bondage and freeing your family to live in a healthy way. That, to me, is worth it all!

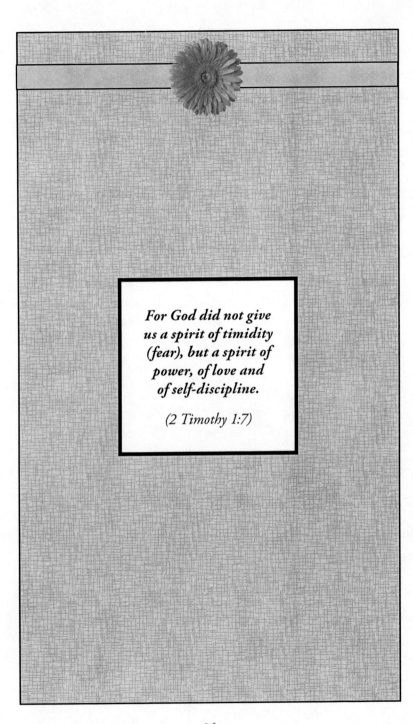

For God did not give us a spirit of timidity (fear), but a spirit of power, of love and of self-discipline.

(2 Timothy 1:7)

20

FEAR

There's a curious observation I've made about both women and men. They both have many fears. It seems no matter whom I talk to, everyone fears something or someone. Over the years, God has shown me areas of my life where fear has dominated and shaped me. Learning to recognize and confess my fears to God has helped me grow up in my faith and given me a glimpse of what Jesus called "the abundant life."

There's a story in Mark, chapter 5, that has intrigued me on this journey God has put both Tom and I. In it, Jesus encounters a woman who has been bleeding for many years. She finds the courage within herself to seek Him out and find her physical and spiritual healing. In verse 26 it says, "She had suffered a great deal under the care of many doctors and had spent all she had, yet instead of getting better, she grew worse." So, she finds Jesus and touches his garment. Now, the next verse is amazing because it says, she touched His cloak because she thought, "If I just touch His clothes, I WILL BE HEALED." (emphasis added)

Here's a woman who has suffered many years. She's sought out doctors who have tried but failed to heal her. She's out of money yet she tries one more thing: she goes to the *Master Healer*. The Word says that IMMEDIATELY, not six weeks or ten years, but at once she "felt in her body that she was **freed** from her suffering."

In this walk called "Recovery," I have met many women who feel they are suffering under the oppressions of addiction in their lives. I have seen men who are suffering under the load of guilt and shame because of their acting out. The parallel in both men and women is that both are tired of seeking answers to their pain but instead of getting better, they are growing worse.

Like the woman who tried one more time to find healing, I believe millions are longing for something to set them free. Almost as if it were peanut butter and jelly, the hope of abundant life and fear go hand in hand. At the core of almost conversation I've had is fear: fear of failure, fear of being alone, fear of abandonment, fear of raising their children alone, fear of rejection and fear of the illusive and most powerful "What ifs?" Oh, don't get me wrong: everyone wants to be free, but unfortunately, it is fear that keeps them from that reality.

For men, they are afraid they aren't enough whether we're talking about their marriage, their masculinity or in their careers. They fear they won't succeed, or if they do succeed they won't be able to maintain that success once they achieve it. They, like their wives, are prisoner to their fears and if they try to find healing especially from their sexual addiction "one more time," they just might fail. So fear becomes the inhibitor, the excuse of so many men *and women* as to why they don't seek recovery or stay with it.

What is interesting to me is just *why* all of us, especially those who know Jesus and read our Bibles, why are we so afraid? Looking further on this passage in Mark, I believe Jesus can teach all of us something that's valuable to breaking free from the stronghold of fear. In verses 35-36, the story continues after Jesus liberates the sick woman from her suffering. In these verses, we see how the father of a dieing girl is told that she has died. His "friends" tell him not to bother with Jesus. "She's dead." Oh, how I love Jesus in these verses! He "ignores" all the rhetoric and all the excuses buzzing around him and cuts to the chase! He says, "Don't be afraid; just believe."

"Don't be afraid. Just believe." Jesus is calling us to believe that He really is more powerful than our strongest fears, able to heal our deepest wounds, and more desirable to our thirsty souls than any pseudo lover. In our fears, we struggle to breathe deeply of God's sufficiency. Held captive, we wrestle against the "what ifs" of life and we spin in our insane cycles. All the while, Jesus beckons us, "Don't be afraid. Just believe."

In the Word, Jesus is: the lover of our souls, sufficient, almighty, our healer in the emotional, physical and spiritual realms, unconditional lover, our heavenly husband, our dream maker, enough, our keeper, protector, provider, sustainer, King, Savior, friend, companion. He is the beginning AND the end and we are lovingly held in the sweet in-between.

So what are we so afraid of? God is teaching me when I believe all that Jesus says of Himself I cannot camp out in fear any longer. I am compelled to risk everything, trusting that He is my all in all. Then, truly I can say, I am living the abundant life that Jesus came to give. "Don't fear; just believe."

Facing Your Hippos This Week:

Fear is a crippling, dominating force that can dominate our lives if we allow it to do so. If we are to walk in recovery, it is one hippo that we must face. This week as you meditate on the Word and spend time in prayer, journal those fears that you are experiencing. Be honest. Be aware of how you may be reacting to life instead of proactively walking with Christ in the abundant life. Take your cares to Jesus and think about WHY you are afraid. Look at the list in the paragraph above that states some of the attributes of Jesus. Ask God what characteristic about Him you need to *believe* in order for you to walk out of your fears and into freedom. Remember: Jesus is patiently waiting with His hand outstretched and He is ready to meet your deepest needs.

And this is my prayer: that your love may abound more and more in knowledge and depth of insight, so that you may be able to discern what is best and may be pure and blameless until the day of Christ.

(Philippians 1:9-10)

21
TRUST YOUR GUT!

It has been thirteen years since we lived in Jacksonville, Arkansas. It seems like only a short time has passed and yet, much has happened in that time. We've lived in Apple Valley and Lakeville, Minnesota and Tennessee, been a part of four different churches and made many friends along the way. Much has changed for our family of five, including our once-young girls, who are now in college and high school. One thing that hasn't changed, though, regardless of how many moves or places we've lived is my memory of Arkansas. It has always been shrouded with a sort of sadness, a black cloud, if you will, over the canopy of my mind where happiness just can't seem to permeate.

Last year, 2009, as Tom entered his sixth year of recovery work and of practicing a lifestyle of being more open and honest with me, he came in one morning and told me he wanted to talk to me. In the past, comments like that would have wreaked havoc on my intestinal tract, but thanks to recovery, I whispered a surrendering prayer and welcomed his transparency.

Tom confessed that when we lived in Arkansas, it was the worst three years of his addiction. My mind flooded back to those years and I remember thinking, "No wonder I felt crazy!" Tom told me that after we had Victoria, he started viewing porn on a regular and compulsive basis. He shared how on his lunch hour, he would leave the building where he worked and would go to the classrooms where he spent his evenings three nights a week for his master's degree, take porn movies, and spend the time acting out in his addiction. I remembered that time in our marriage as being so weird. I knew something wasn't right but I couldn't put my finger on it. There was no evidence of any wrongdoing other than a sick feeling in my gut that has haunted me for the last decade. Honestly, when Tom told me these things, I felt vindicated. I wasn't crazy after all!

If I've learned anything about myself over the last several years in recovery, it is that God has given women a sixth sense. We are blessed, though some may feel cursed, with an ability to know or discern when things are not right in life. We may not know the details, but for a lot of women, we can sense that something is amiss. Over the course of the last six years, God has affirmed this truth in me. It was shortly after Tom's revelation about his addiction being in full swing some 12 years prior in Arkansas that we visited a new Sunday school class in our church in Tennessee. We had no idea going in why we had picked this class but knew without a doubt after it was over. The teacher stood, and I'll never forget what he said, "Well, class, I prepared a lesson all week and this morning I really feel like God wants me to say something to you, so I'm going to forego the planned lesson and share something with you." He went on to say to the men of the class of the importance of keeping their minds pure and how he had struggled with emotional affairs. He went on to share how easy it is for men (and women) to go too far in their thought processes and how we must guard our minds against that.

I thought it was a good lesson that needed to be taught, but didn't think much more about it. Later the next day, Tom came into the kitchen and wanted to talk. He went on to confess that the years when we lived in Germany, he had had an emotional affair with the lady that he had spent so much time staring at during church socials and telling me he had felt sorry. All those years of feeling so sure something was going on in Tom's mind with this other woman finally came to the Light, because of a Sunday school teacher's obedience. Now, this revelation made me feel a sense of God's perfect timing and of his love for me.

I believe that as women we are taught inadvertently in our society that we are just being "paranoid," "overly sensitive," "ridiculous," even "crazy" when we question the gut feelings we have. Think about the last time you had an uneasy feeling about a situation, and you told someone. I'll bet there's a good chance you were laughed at or at best, just given a pat on the hand and told, "Oh, now you don't *know* that to be true." It has been my experience with other wives of sexual addicts that many times, we are absolutely right with our premonitions and our deepest feelings. I've heard many wives say they just didn't feel like everything was right in their marriages. But, they either wouldn't ask their husbands the hard questions or, if they did ask, they would get answers claiming innocence, which only left the wives feeling crazier. One thing I've learned through recovery: we have the *right and responsibility* to speak our truth and ask questions if something is bothering us. If we don't, then we are really cheating ourselves out of the satisfaction that comes with speaking truth and letting our husbands know our heart's desires. We are *powerless* over whether or not they tell us the truth, but we can find peace in our souls from confronting those fears that haunt us and that sit in our guts inflicting not only emotional pain but physical pain as well.

When you are married to someone who is not being honest with you because of the shame they feel due to their unfaithful behavior, it creates a sort of craziness in your normal day-to-day life. This atmosphere can cause you to feel there is *no one* you can fully trust or believe. I guess the question for wives of sexual addicts becomes, "What are **you** going to do to live in truth and walk in integrity in your marriage?" Because we are powerless over our husband's addictions, we have to take the mature stance by confronting them in love when we feel in our guts that something is wrong.

If I had had the wisdom to ask Tom about his addiction during the time we lived in Arkansas, it may or may not have reaped truthful answers. But the difference in my marriage would have been that he would have known what I was feeling and that I was seeking truth.

Then, the feeling in my gut would have been exposed to the Light and at least I could have rested in knowing I had asked my husband the hard questions I held in the deepest place of my heart. There's something very powerful about taking responsibility in our lives and speaking truth to our husbands and to others out of genuine love and concern for our relationship. I believe God honors that and will bless us for our sincere attempts to walk in truth.

Facing Your Hippos This Week:

Starting today, become more conscious of what you're thinking and what you are feeling especially in your intestinal area (the gut). When a "gut feeling" overcomes you, write it down in your journal. Begin to ask God to show you areas in your thinking and feeling that need to be confronted and discussed with your husband or others. If you feel there is something that just isn't right and needs to be addressed, pray about it first. Seek godly counsel if you need to, then speak your truth and trust your gut!

Humble yourselves, therefore, under God's mighty hand, that he may lift you up in due time. Cast all your anxiety on him because he cares for you.

(1 Peter 5:6-7)

22

CAST THEM AWAY

My Grandpa Lloyd was a great fisherman and was full of wonderful stories about the many fish he had caught. Often he would visit our farm in Illinois and we'd go fishing at the pond, sometimes 'til the sun would set and the mosquitoes would come a bitin'. One thing he taught me was how to cast my bait into the water. The skill required holding the fishing pole parallel to the ground and then reaching back over my right shoulder with my fishing arm fully extended. Back, back, my arm would reach, and then, slowly, I would give the line a heave ho! Sometimes my wiggly worm would go flying way out into the pond and I'd smile with glee. At other times, the worm and hook would get stuck in a nearby tree or clump of grass and would never make it into the water. I learned, though, that if I focused and was intentional with my casting, the worm would soon be airborne, land in the pond where I wanted it to, and with a little time and God's blessing, a fish would nibble.

It's the same way with life and walking with the Lord. It has been over eight years since we left Minnesota and since receiving the scathing letter that ignited our recovery journey. I now have the advantage of looking back and seeing how God has worked in our lives to mold and shape us. Just like he has always done in my life, God has faithfully used every moment and every situation to guide us. I know now more clearly than ever, that the Creator of the universe, *Elohim*, has a perfect plan for my life and for my husband. In his plan, God has used the most unsuspecting persons and situations to teach me his ways.

In Jeremiah 29:11 it says, "For I know the plans I have for you," declares the LORD, "plans to prosper you and not to harm you, plans to give you hope and a future." If it is true that God has a "perfect plan" for my life, then that belief system helps me to see God's sovereign hand guiding me through the storms of my life. Tom's addiction and subsequent affairs of the heart hurt. The letter and rejection from the small group hurt, but God used those circumstances to teach me just how much I needed him to be **LORD** of my life and to show me his will for our lives. God began teaching me about that plan as I began to seek him first every day.

About a year after we moved to Tennessee, I facilitated a women's Bible study in our home entitled, *The Confident Woman* by Anabel Gillham. As we began to delve into the truths of that book, the eyes of my heart began to open. God showed me something I had never seen before in His Word and it literally changed my life.

The subtitle of the book is *Knowing Who You Are in Christ*. This idea of knowing who I truly was intrigued me. For most of my life I was the singer, the cute little "King's Kid," the smart one in school, the runner-up to Homecoming Queen, and the worldly list went on and on, yet in my deepest parts I didn't really see myself as God does. I measured my worth by the world's standards, by accomplishments, and by what other people said of me.

God used this study to show me how much he loved me and how trustworthy his Word is for my life. One of the quotes from the book was this:

> *"What God wants you to be does not depend on your circumstances, the people around you, your talents, your gifts, or on making a right turn when you should have turned left. The world uses these very same things to control us, to defeat us, to squeeze us into its mold. But God will use them to fit us into His mold, to conform us into His image, to transform us into all He wants us to be. God is not nearly as interested in changing our circumstances as He is in changing US in our circumstances."*

For most of my life, I had depended more on my God-given talents than on the God who gave me the talents. And, do you know what? That worked for me for a long, long time. But, like an old pair of blue jeans that once fit perfectly, if you lose or gain weight, well, the old doesn't fit anymore. It sounds crazy, but it was *because of* the revelation of Tom's addiction that I began to realize I couldn't rely on the things I had once relied and God began revealing just how many false idols and how many things I had been using in my quest to find true intimacy with Him. God brought me to my knees and I began to learn what it means to see his sufficiency in the midst of my circumstances and just how much I needed him more than Tom or anybody else. God was beginning to teach me what it means to surrender my cares upon Him, to fully rely on *Him* for everything, and to really embrace the truth that He loves me *unconditionally.*

In 1 Peter 5:7, it states to cast your cares upon him, because he cares for you. Having a husband who struggled with a sexual addiction was an emotional "care." Having to raise three young daughters alone was an ongoing and at times, overwhelming "care." At times, feeling lonely, afraid, hurt, ashamed, and sad were all "cares." So, I began to learn that in **all** things, Jesus beckons us to throw our cares upon him and stop hanging onto them and obsessing over them. Why? Because he *cares for us.*

So, I began to do just that: I began each and every day by casting my cares upon Him. I baited my line. I put my character flaws, my weaknesses, my husband's addiction, my children, and other people on the hook. Then, with all the intentionality and focus I could muster, in Jesus' name, I would cast them away to the One who is more than able to accomplish what I cannot. I began making a choice—not just every morning but every minute of every day—to trust God, to take my cares to him, so I could rest in the peace that only he can give. I would often catch myself reeling my cares back in and wrestling with them all over again. To be more aware of my feelings and to cast them upon the Lord as soon as I was cognizant of them felt like work at first. But, soon

I learned to cast them away and leave them with Him. I would cast them away, cast them away, cast them away.

Cast them away.

 Facing Your Hippos This Week:

Here's a fun visual activity from Anabel Gilham's book, *The Confident Woman.* Purchase a helium balloon in your favorite color. When you get home, find some quiet time and begin asking God to reveal to you any cares that are weighing you down and keeping you from living the abundant life. These cares might include: wounds from your past that you haven't dealt with, or today's feelings of anger, sadness, hurt, fear, loneliness, guilt, shame, and unforgiveness.

As the Holy Spirit speaks to you, take a Sharpie and begin writing on the helium balloon all the "cares" of your heart. When you are finished writing, take your balloon outside, hold it out at arm's length, and recite 1 Peter 5:7, "Cast all your cares on Him because He cares for you." You might even want to thank Jesus for being willing to take all of your cares upon him. Then, when you feel ready to *let go,* release the balloon, along with the cares you have written on it, and watch it ascend to heaven. Let your cares go and trust God to faithfully take them from you.

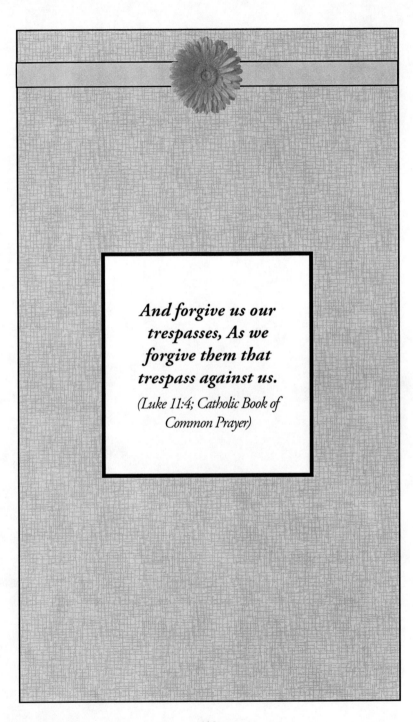

And forgive us our trespasses, As we forgive them that trespass against us.

(Luke 11:4; Catholic Book of Common Prayer)

23
FORGIVENESS

Back in 1992, when we lived in North Carolina, I wrote a song entitled "Forgiveness." The full understanding of what forgiveness means, is clearer to me now than it has ever been and the challenge of just how to truly do it is still something I am learning to do well. God is good that way. He brings us into the Light of his truth at just the right time—his time. The words to that song are:

Help me, Lord Jesus, to forgive.
Help me, Lord Jesus, to understand
All have sinned and **all** fall short
Of your Holy Plan.
Help me, Lord Jesus, to embrace
How much that you love me,
Oh, Amazing Grace!
Help me to see
You're all I need each and every day!

Forgiveness of my fellow man
It sets me free!
It helps me live my life the way it
Ought to be

Forgiveness helps me see
The love of the Father in me!
Oh, LORD, help me with Forgiveness!

Help me, Lord Jesus, to let go
Of hurt and disappointment
That cloud my way
Help me to be Your Light shining
Each and every day.

When I think of what Christ did for all of humanity on Calvary, the fact that he "bore all of our sins" on the tree, I am compelled to look at my circumstances and others who have wronged me with less judgment and more compassion. By nature, it is not easy to forgive those who trespass against us. I struggled with this dilemma for a long time, even years after both Tom and I started doing some hard work on our issues. It wasn't long before the Holy Spirit revealed to me that as long as I allow the memories of others' trespasses against me to haunt and have authority over me, I will never be free.

So the question I began asking was this: "Lord, how do I forgive those who trespass against me and how do I truly forgive myself?" This is a big one because, honestly, to hold on to the memory of the hurts and wrongs done to me falsely gives me "ammunition" to hate them back. Similarly, by holding on to past blunders, in a way, I can become consumed with hating myself instead of moving on to bigger and better things for God's glory.

Jesus taught us something revolutionary when it comes to forgiveness. He said to *forgive* those who trespass against us—seventy times seven (Matthew 18:22). Not only that, but while he hung on the cross, bleeding to death with the weight of our sin on his shoulders, he asked the heavenly Father to forgive those who had wronged Him. Why? Jesus said, "Because they do not **know** what they are doing" (Luke 23:34).

Wow! They do not *know* what they are doing. This verse has helped me to look at forgiving others with more hope than I ever thought possible. In chapter twenty-four, "What Exactly is Sexual

Addiction and Codependency?" I have listed some statistical information regarding studies that have been done that equate the high an addict gets from looking at porn with the high a drug addict gets when he snorts cocaine ("The Brain Science Behind Internet Pornography Addiction," www.candeocan.com). If I look at my husband's addiction with the knowledge that he didn't do it intentionally, then I can begin to understand what Jesus said and modeled for us on the cross. That doesn't mean I excuse Tom's behavior or that I push the hippo under the rug. No, I am not saying that. Rather, I am saying, I can **choose** to forgive Tom for his trespasses against me and against the vow he made to me on our wedding day. By doing so, I am then freed from the burden of hurt his choices, through the addiction, have caused.

Also, I have had to learn to forgive myself for making mistakes. Here's some transparency for you! I am a recovering perfectionist. I still struggle sometimes with the temptation to do everything as close to perfect as possible. For example: Within my marriage, I've had to forgive myself for enabling Tom and allowing our circumstances to swallow up my dreams. I allowed denial and minimizing to dictate our marriage relationship for years while choosing not to seek professional help. I also allowed myself to become so enmeshed in the "hippo game" that I lost myself. I can now look back and see that I was an enabling, codependent wife. By forgiving myself and by recognizing my own weaknesses, I began to see clearly the plank of wood in my own eye, instead of focusing my attention and energy on Tom's issues. Jesus said it best when he warned us to look at our own issues and deal with them first before we look at other's faults. I am not suggesting that my sin caused Tom's choices. On the contrary! What I have learned is that Jesus came to save me from my sins just as much as He came to save Tom from his.

One specific time, I asked God to show me my own areas of sin that I needed to address. (One word of advice if you do this: make sure you are lying down on the couch. This can be pretty overwhelming!) After several days of being bombarded with examples, the Holy Spirit began to show me my need for Christ and His forgiveness was and is just as great as Tom's need for a Savior.

Could it be that the key to living the victorious and abundant life that Jesus came to give us lies in our willingness to forgive others and ourselves? I don't have it within myself to forgive others, but Jesus' power, his Holy Spirit in me is *more than able* to empower me to forgive. There are just some hurts that are too painful. Thinking about my husband looking at nude pictures of other women and the fact that he did not remain true to our marriage vows hurts more than delivering a baby without a pain killer. The stinging rejection from those who I thought were my friends makes my heart ache all over again, if I let it. Owning my codependency and realizing I could have spoken up and done something sooner if I hadn't allowed fear to rule in my life is hard to swallow. In order for me to be free, though, I *must* forgive others and myself and walk forward, instead of living in the past.

I am powerless over life's overwhelming, heart-breaking circumstances and over the consequences of my own poor choices. By allowing Christ's power to help me forgive others and myself, I am free! By releasing those who have hurt me from the debt or apology that may *never* come, I allow the Holy Spirit's power to reign in my heart. I also begin to see others as much in need of a Savior as I am. When I look at it that way, it changes me from the inside out and helps me to find Christ's power in a whole new way.

One of the best definitions of why we need to forgive can be found in the book, *Wild at Heart* by John Eldridge. God has taught me the importance of forgiving others who have sinned against me, including myself and in so doing, I've learned and continue to learn what it means to live the *abundant* life that Jesus came to give.

Time has come for us to forgive our fathers. Paul warns us that unforgiveness and bitterness can wreck our lives and the lives of others (Eph. 4:31; Heb. 12:15). I am sorry to think of all the years my wife endured the anger and bitterness that I redirected at her from my father. As someone has said, forgiveness is setting a prisoner free and then discovering the prisoner was you. I found some help in Bly's experience of forgiving his own father, when he said, "I began to think of him not as someone who had deprived me of love or attention or companionship, but as someone who himself had been deprived, by his father and his mother and by the culture." My father had his own wound that no one ever offered to heal. His father was an alcoholic, too, for a time, and there were some hard years for my dad as a young man just as there were for me.

Now you must understand: Forgiveness is a choice. It is not a feeling, but an act of the will. As Neil Anderson has written, "Don't wait to forgive until you feel like forgiving; you will never get there. Feelings take time to heal after the choice to forgive is made." We allow God to bring the hurt up from our past, for "if your forgiveness doesn't visit the emotional core of your life, it will be incomplete." We acknowledge that it hurt, that it mattered, and we choose to extend forgiveness to our father. This is *not* saying, "It didn't really matter"; it is *not* saying, "I probably deserved part of it anyway."

Forgiveness says, "It was wrong, it mattered, and I release you." And then we ask God to father us, and to tell us our true name.

(Wild at Heart, 131–132)

Facing Your Hippos This Week:

Look in the back of your Bible in the concordance section. Write down every verse on forgiveness and unforgiveness. I've listed a few of my favorites. I have these on a sheet of purple paper that is prominently placed in my bedroom where I can read over them and be reminded of the importance of forgiveness and also the possibility that *with Christ* I **can** forgive others and even myself!

I've included some of my favorites below. Make your own list, adding to these, if you'd like and post it in a prominent place in your home, workplace or car. The Word says that we are to "think on" things that are pure and lovely. When we choose to do so, our minds are transformed.

Forgiveness/Unforgiveness Scriptures:

2 Chronicles 7:14 If my people, who are called by my name, will humble themselves and pray and seek my face and turn from their wicked ways, then will I hear from heaven and will forgive their sin and will heal their land.

Matthew 5:43-46a You have heard that it was said, "Love your neighbor and hate your enemy." But I tell you: Love your enemies and pray for those who persecute you, that you may be sons of your Father in heaven. He causes his sun to rise on the evil and the good, and sends rain on the righteous and the unrighteous. If you love those who love you, what reward will you get?

Matthew 6:9-15 This, then, is how you should pray: " 'Our Father in heaven, hallowed be your name, your kingdom come, your will be done on earth as it is in heaven. Give us today our daily bread. Forgive us our debts, as we also have forgiven our debtors. And lead us not into temptation but deliver us from the evil one, for yours is the kingdom and the power and the glory forever. For if you forgive men when they sin against you, your heavenly Father will also forgive you. *But* if you do not forgive men their sins, your Father will not forgive your sins. (emphasis added)

Matthew 18:21-22 Then Peter came to Jesus and asked, "Lord, how many times shall I forgive my brother when he sins against me? Up to seven times? Jesus answered, "I tell you, not seven times, but seventy-seven times."

John 20:21-23 Again Jesus said, "Peace be with you! As the Father has sent me, I am sending you." And with that he breathed on them and said, "Receive the Holy Spirit. If you forgive anyone his sins, they are forgiven; if you do not forgive them, they are not forgiven."

Colossians 3:12-13 – Therefore, as God's chosen people, holy and dearly loved, clothe yourselves with compassion, kindness, humility, gentleness and patience. Bear with each other and forgive whatever grievances you may have against one another. Forgive as the Lord forgave you.

1 John 1:9-2:2 If we confess our sins, he is faithful and just and will forgive us our sins and purify us from all unrighteousness. If we claim we have not sinned, we make him out to be a liar and his word has no place in our lives. My dear children, I write this to you so that you will not sin. But if anybody does sin, we have one who speaks to the Father in our defense—Jesus Christ, the Righteous One. He is the atoning sacrifice for our sins, and not only for ours but also for the sins of the whole world.

1 John 2:9-12 Anyone who claims to be in the light but hates his brother is still in the darkness. Whoever loves his brother lives in the light, and there is nothing in him to make him stumble. But whoever hates his brother is in the darkness and walks around in the darkness; he does not know where he is going, because the darkness has blinded him. I write to you, dear children, because your sins have been forgiven on account of his name.

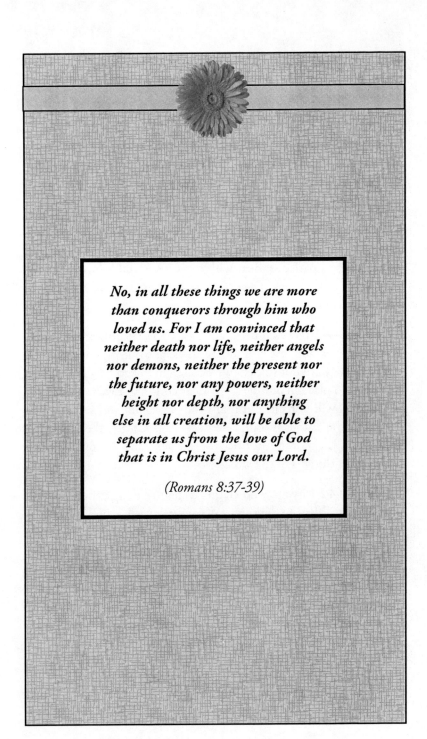

No, in all these things we are more than conquerors through him who loved us. For I am convinced that neither death nor life, neither angels nor demons, neither the present nor the future, nor any powers, neither height nor depth, nor anything else in all creation, will be able to separate us from the love of God that is in Christ Jesus our Lord.

(Romans 8:37-39)

24

WHAT EXACTLY IS SEXUAL ADDICTION AND CODEPENDENCY?

Before Tom and I began to seek professional help for his addiction, I didn't understand what sexual addiction was. I knew what the Bible said about sexual sin and what my upbringing taught me. In addition, as I began to seek professional help with my own issues, I learned that some of my ways of coping with life were unhealthy. I learned that some of my belief systems were what professionals would call codependent. The best definition I can think of to describe codependency is instead of being proactive in my life I was reactive to others' behaviors, words, and so on.

When I began writing this book, I talked with women in similar situations and realized I needed a lot of questions answered and so did they. In an effort to understand, I began to research sexual addiction and codependency. I believe now that if I know what I'm up against, that knowledge can change my life as well as others! The following are some definitions that I found helpful in understanding sexual addiction. This article is taken from Faithful and True Ministries Website and is used by permission. (www.faithfulandtrueministries.org)

Sexual Addiction:

Patrick Carnes defines sexual addiction as having a pathological relationship with a mood altering chemical or behavior. Simply stated, sexual addiction is the lack of control of some sexual behavior or relationship. Perhaps the most helpful definition is a practical one: sexual behavior that has a negative effect on one's life. Like with alcohol or drugs, sex addiction fits the classic, four-component model of what comprises an addiction:

1. Compulsivity - The loss of control over a behavior. An addict continues in the behavior or relationship despite repeated attempts to stop.
2. Continuation despite negative consequences.
3. Preoccupation or obsession.
4. Tolerance - More of the same behavior or an escalation of progressive behaviors is required to get the same "high."

Definitions and Behaviors of Sexual Addiction from SASH –

The Society for the Advancement of Sexual Health:

Sexual addiction comes in many different forms. There is no single type of behavior or even amount of behavior that will indicate you are a sexual addict. The problem is much more complex than can be explained in a few words and if you have been living the life of a sex addict, you know how difficult it is to describe what you are experiencing.

Three Basic Things to Consider When You Define Sexual Addiction Are:

1. Do I have a sense that I have lost control over whether or not I engage in my specific out-of-control sexual behavior?

2. Am I experiencing significant consequences because of my specific out-of-control sexual behavior?

3. Do I feel like I am constantly thinking about my specific out-of-control sexual behavior, even when I don't want to?

It is these three "hallmarks" that help to define the boundaries of sexual addiction and compulsivity. The range of behaviors can include masturbation and pornography through sexual exploitation of others. If the three questions are answered yes, then you may want to seek further help to begin to sort out the complexities of your sexual behavior and find out for certain if sexual addiction is the best descriptor of your problem.

Internet (Cybersex) Addiction Checklist

The Cyber Sex Addiction Checklist is a set of questions to help you see your sexual activity more clearly. It is an assessment of sexually compulsive or addictive behavior. A high number of YES answers may be a sign of some issues with sex addiction. After using this questionnaire, please consult a trained professional to discuss these issues further.

1. Spending increasing amounts of online time focused on sexual or romantic intrigue or involvement.

2. Involvement in multiple romantic or sexual affairs in chat rooms, Internet or BBS (Bulletin Boards).

3. Not considering online sexual or romantic "affairs" to be a possible violation of spousal/partnership commitments.

4. Failed attempts to cut back on frequency of online or Internet sexual and romantic involvement or interaction.

5. Online use interferes with work (tired or late due to previous night's use, online while at work, etc.).

6. Online use interferes with primary relationships (e.g., minimizing or lying to partners about online activities, spending less time with family or partners).

7. Intense engagement in collecting Internet pornography.

8. Engaging in fantasy online acts or experiences which would be illegal if carried out (e.g., rape, child molestation).

9. Decreased social or family interactive time due to online fantasy involvements.

10. Being secretive or lying about amount of time spent online or type of sexual/romantic fantasy activities carried out online.

11. Engaging with sexual or romantic partners met online, while also involved in marital or other primary relationship.

12. Increasing complaints and concern from family or friends about the amount of time spent online.

13. Frequently becoming angry or extremely irritable when asked to give up online involvement to engage with partners, family, or friends.

14. Primary focus of sexual or romantic life becomes increasingly related to computer activity (including pornographic CD-ROM use).

This test is used with permission from its author, Rob Weiss, M.A.

Copyright 2007 The Society for the
Advancement of Sexual Health (SASH)

Website by Media A-Team

I've listened to other stories from women who have shared different scenarios in their marriages. Tired of feeling like they must have sex and not knowing how to speak honestly to their mates about their truest feelings, a lot of wives' stories have made me wonder about their husbands and if there are addictions that are being dismissed.

I asked Tom about one lady I knew who shared her story about having to give her husband sex almost every day of the week. He gave me some good insight about what makes an addict one or not.

He went on to say that you have to know the reason *why* he wanted to make love to his wife every night. Was it because he truly loved her and wanted to be one with her or was it a true addiction? Tom then argued that if he *truly* loved his wife, he would have realized that everybody needs a break at least one night a week! Tom then went on to say that if a man feels compelled to have sex that often and if *he can't stop himself,* then that's a red flag that there may be a problem.

One of the most helpful truths I have discovered in our recovery work is that Tom's addiction wasn't about me or about me not having enough sex with him. Whoa! Was that ever a load off when I learned that one! His addiction was all about Tom trying to *medicate* some pain, some wound deep inside of him. It was not about me at all. It was about him not knowing how to deal with his anger, hurt, shame, sadness, fear, guilt, or his loneliness and using false "lovers" to make him think he was okay, even if for a brief moment.

Sexual addiction is also something that some are now finding in scientific studies to have the same affect on the brain that cocaine or other hard-core drugs have. What started out at the young age of eleven or twelve for Tom and his brothers looking at *Playboy* became a thirty year stronghold. Looking at pornography can have the same affects on the brain that LSD or opium or any drug can. Anna Rose Childress, of the University of Pennsylvania, does brain imaging studies and says. "Sex addicts resemble cocaine addicts and probably share with them a defect in inhibitory circuitry. In both instances, people say when they're in this big 'go' state they feel as though there is override [of inhibition]…a feeling of being unable to stop." Peter Martin of Vanderbilt University in Nashville, Tennessee, says that a "preliminary study with normal subjects indicates that brain activity associated with sexual arousal looks like that accompanying drug consumption."

(http://www.sciencemag.org/cgi/content/full/294/5544/980)

Howard Shaffer, who heads the Division on Addictions at Harvard University says, "I had great difficulty with my own colleagues when I suggested that a lot of addiction is the result of experience...repetitive, high-emotion, high-frequency experience." Some of the reasons that led Shaffer to this viewpoint are the facts that "sex addicts do display behaviors characteristic of addiction: They obsess over whatever their favorite practice is, never get enough, feel out of control, and experience serious disruption of their lives because of it." These behaviors have led Mr. Shaffer to conclude that they qualify as sex addictions. "I think those things that are robust and reliable shifters of subjective experience all hold the potential for addiction." (www.sciencemag.org)

One thing I am thankful for throughout the seventeen years of our marriage is that Tom never once coerced me to have sex when I didn't want to. I am grateful that my husband did respect me enough to never ask me to engage in any activity that compromised my values. I am also grateful to God that he never crossed the "skin threshold," being physically intimate with another women. His stronghold was in the emotional realm and in masturbation. For this, I am grateful, but I know many other wives whose husbands have had multiple affairs, prostitutes, and see nothing harmful about their lifestyle choices. I also know there are millions of wives who live with the gut feeling that there is something not right in their marriages and who want to find some answers to the questions of their hearts.

Codependency:

A word that has become familiar by authors like Melody Beattie and Mia Mellody is *codependency*. Back in 1992, when Tom and I first started seeing a professional counselor in North Carolina, I was given that title. At first, it offended me, but now I can honestly say it fit me to a tee. The best definition I can give to you about this personality type is found in Melody Beattie's book, *"Codependent No More." "*A codependent person is one who has let another person's behavior affect him or her, and who is obsessed with controlling that person's behavior." What that means to me is that a person who has these tendencies will be *reactionary*, meaning they react to others' behaviors, words and influence on their lives. A person who is not codependent will be a *proactive* person, meaning they allow others to say, act, or think whatever they choose and it won't cause the healthy person to react.

Looking back over the years, I can see how my belief system of codependent tendencies was the foundation of many reactionary moments. Instead of living and walking in confidence based on God's opinion of me and his truths about me, I spent many hours, days, and even weeks "spinning" (reacting to) what others did or did not do to me. Oh, the hours I've wasted in the past worrying and fretting over whether or not others would call or invite me to parties or if Tom would notice this or that! Codependency demands that my energy and time be wasted on situations that I have no control over, yet that consume me. Learning to identify these tendencies and the "why" behind them has helped me to become a proactive person, instead of a codependent one.

When I started attending support groups for "wives like me," I saw a similarity in a lot of the women in the group. It was interesting to see how such beautiful women on the exterior battled so many emotional demons on the inside. Of all the things God has allowed me to see as a result of our recovery journey, I have to say that understanding codependent tendencies has been one of my favorites. By learning what these common characteristics are and by exchanging the lies in my head for truth, I've been set free and my family has been as well.

The following is a list of some of the most common codependent tendencies. I Googled codependent characteristics and compiled this list from several lists I found. It is by no means, exhaustive, but rather is a sampling of some of the most universal tendencies.

Characteristics of Codependent People

- An exaggerated sense of responsibility for the actions of others

- A tendency to confuse love and pity, with the tendency to "love" people they can pity and rescue

- A tendency to do more than their share, all of the time

- A tendency to become hurt when people don't recognize their efforts

- An unhealthy dependence on relationships. The codependent will do anything to hold on to a relationship—to avoid the feeling of abandonment

- An extreme need for approval and recognition

- A sense of guilt when asserting themselves

- A compelling need to control others

- Lack of trust in self and/or others

- Fear of being abandoned or alone

- Difficulty identifying feelings

- Rigidity/difficulty adjusting to change

- Problems with intimacy/boundaries

- Chronic anger

- Lying/dishonesty

- Poor communications

- Difficulty making decisions

Some Questions to Think About

1. Do you keep quiet to avoid arguments?

2. Are you always worried about others' opinions of you?

3. Have you ever lived with someone with an alcohol or drug problem?

4. Have you ever lived with someone who hits or belittles you?

5. Are the opinions of others more important than your own?

6. Do you have difficulty adjusting to changes at work or home?

7. Do you feel rejected when significant others spend time with friends?

8. Do you doubt your ability to be who you want to be?

9. Are you uncomfortable expressing your true feelings to others?

10. Have you ever felt inadequate?

11. Do you feel like a "bad person" when you make a mistake?

12. Do you have difficulty taking compliments or gifts?

13. Do you feel humiliation when your child or spouse makes a mistake?

14. Do you think people in your life would go downhill without your constant efforts?

15. Do you frequently wish someone could help you get things done?

16. Do you have difficulty talking to people in authority, such as the police or your boss?

17. Are you confused about who you are or where you are going with your life?

18. Do you have trouble saying "no" when asked for help?

19. Do you have trouble asking for help?

20. Do you have so many things going at once that you can't do justice to any of them?

Again, the goal in looking at these lists is not to shame or blame you or anyone you know. I want to encourage you to read these lists with an attitude of gaining knowledge so that you can change if you need to and grow as a person. I think all of us feel bad if we make mistakes. However, a codependent person will make a mistake and then for the next month or even year, will beat themselves up for it. A healthy person realizes we are finite creatures who make mistakes and that's *okay!*

 Facing Your Hippos This Week:

Take the list of questions above and spend some time this week asking yourself if you have any of these tendencies on a regular basis. When you finish that list, go ahead and read through the characteristics of codependent people. In your quiet time, ask God to help you begin to recognize when you are acting or reacting in codependent ways. When you recognize it, immediately tell God about it, asking Him to help you to replace the negative tendency with a positive one. Remember: you are fearfully and wonderfully made in the image of God. When you believe God's truth about you, you will not be codependent on other's opinions of you! Instead, you will be *dependent* on God's perspective of you, living proactively as a confident woman who knows she is loved fully.

"What does it mean to 'be present' in the lives of others? Perhaps it has something to do with listening with our hearts and not just our ears, dismissing our own seemingly important agendas and instead, sitting at someone's feet risking to care. This, too, can only take place when each person has chosen emotional, spiritual and physical health for themselves first, enabling them to love fully and deeply. To find a mate and a lover, in fact, to BE a mate and a lover who will risk 'showing up,' well, this is a rare find, indeed."

~Kolinda Duer

25
THE "SHOW-UP PLACE"

When I attended the Bethesda Workshop for Spouses of Addicts, one of our speakers was a man who had been married to a sex addict. Unfortunately, their marriage ended in divorce, but instead of spending the rest of his life regretting what had been or what could have been, he chose to become healthy, emotionally. One of the things he shared with our group was what he called, "The Show-Up Place."

He told us that for many years, he had been paralyzed by the fact that his wife was an addict. He became so concerned about her whereabouts, her actions, and behaviors that he lost himself in her "stuff." By learning about himself and by getting professional help, he was able to be present, to "show up" in his daily life situations.

What this means is this: when we are consumed by fear that our spouses are going to lust or cheat on us, or by insecurity that we are not good enough, most of our mental energy is diverted from our own lives and is consumed by their actions (or lack thereof). The first step of Alcoholics Anonymous and Sexaholics Anonymous groups states that we are powerless over other people's addictions...over *our* addictions and tendencies.

If it's true (and it is) that I am powerless over my husband and his choices, then I have two choices I can make (Yes, I do have some power over a few things in my life!): either I can fret and worry and spend my every waking moment thinking, "What if he..." (like I did in Germany) **or** I can acknowledge I am powerless over Tom's choices and actions and implement the second step of Alcoholics Anonymous which calls us to believe in a higher power that is able to handle Tom far better than me. By surrendering Tom over to God, who is more than able to do what I need him to do (Ephesians 3:20), I am free to focus my energy on my own life and the work that I need to do to walk with Christ (and believe me, it's a full time job!). Suddenly, instead of being consumed with Tom, I'm free to "show up" and engage in other's lives because I'm available to them.

"So How Do I Show Up?" You ask.

1. **Recognize** what you're obsessing over or what has "triggered" you. The more we learn to be honest about our true feelings, the easier this step will become. This obsessing may be anything from feeling a sense of "craziness" or feeling out of control. I am learning to recognize this sensation when it happens. I go back in my mind, replay conversations I have had, recall what took place in my surroundings and then pinpoint the feelings I'm having and address them. For example, I ask myself, "What are you feeling? What is it you need, Kolinda?" This sounds silly, but is revolutionary for those of us codependents who aren't good at knowing ourselves. Then, when I pinpoint my true feelings, such as hurt, sadness, loneliness, or fear, I honor that feeling and try to find a way to meet the need in my heart.

2. **Confess** that feeling, anxiety or care to God. Cast it upon him because he cares for you and because he can handle your husband or any situation (1 Peter 5:7). This step requires *trust*! The Word tells us to cast or throw our cares upon Jesus. Why? He *cares* for us. God cares that you are feeling scared or angry or sad or lonely or guilty or shamed or glad or hurt. He wants us to tell him about it and to *trust* him to handle life's situation. Has your husband or friend hurt your feelings? Tell Jesus about your hurt. Honor the pain. Cast it up to Jesus and leave it with him who is more than able to handle it. Then, go and talk to your husband or friend and share your true feelings.

3. **Give thanks** that God is able to take your cares upon himself. (Remember the balloons? Let those cares go up, up, up and away!) Every time a care comes up again in my head, I thank God he has it all under his control. The Word says, "But thanks be to God! He gives us the victory through our Lord Jesus Christ." (1 Cor. 15:57). A prayer you could pray to our Father is this:*"Thank you, God, that you have taken my cares and that you know what is best for my life. I trust you and thank you that you are doing something I cannot do for myself. In Jesus' name, amen."*

Let me give you an example of this: I have always become nervous around people who are quiet and reserved. This situation taps into my co-dependent need to "fill in the silence" with chatter. I have learned to recognize when I'm starting to feel anxious around this personality type. First thing I do is acknowledge that I'm fearful that I won't be "enough" to fill in the silence. Next, I honor the feeling of fear. Yep, I'm scared. Then, I ask myself, "What's the truth, Kolinda?" I then go to the truth of God's word which states I am fearfully and wonderfully made in the image of an Almighty Creator and I am enough! Secondly, it's absolutely OK to have some silence when you are conversing with people. I don't have to try and be perfect and make the situation comfortable by rambling on about things I really don't want to talk about, all in an effort to please the other person!

This has revolutionized my life! I can actually eat my salad across the table from a reserved person and wait for the next quality piece of conversation to come up. It's great! And, every time I do this, I have ended up making a friend because I've allowed them to be themselves while I allowed my own personality to just "be"!

Jesus said, "I have come that they may have life, and have it to the full" (John 10:10b). I fully believe that God's ultimate plan for each of our lives as wives of sex addicts, whether they choose recovery or not, is to fully rely on his power working within us to overcome our greatest anxieties, hurts, and sadness. The only way we can walk in the freedom and fullness that Christ brings is to recognize our need for a Savior, confess our weaknesses to him and our need for forgiveness while thankfully acknowledging his faithfulness to meet our deepest longings and needs. By doing so, we can then truly *show up* in the lives of others each and every day.

 Facing Your Hippos This Week:

Have you ever felt like your head was so full of worries and cares that you couldn't even be present in the lives of others? Have your thoughts been all consuming and literally kept you from focusing on the moment? Well, I have and in the recovery world, this is called "spinning." It's that feeling of utter chaos when something untrue or unhealthy has gotten your head and your heart's attention.

I've been working on "doing the hard work of becoming whole on my own" for several years now. I wish I could say I don't spin anymore, but I do. Just this weekend, I got caught up in the whirlwind of fret and down I went. What God has taught me is the importance of asking Him to help me recognize those times when I am "spinning."

This week, try to be aware of times when you allow the circumstances of your life to consume you. When you recognize it happening, stop! Find a quiet place and pray (the bathroom is a great place and make sure you lock the door!) Ask God to help you focus on Him and His peace. Then, confess to him what it is you are feeling. For me, it is usually some fear about something. When you have done that, begin thanking the Lord for His protection over you and your family. By recognizing the situation for what it is, confessing the feelings that are welling up in our hearts and surrendering them to God, we are then able to "show up" in the lives of others in a healthy way.

Friend of a Wounded Heart

Smile--Make 'em think you're happy
Lie--And say that things are fine
And hide that empty longing that you feel
Don't ever show it
Just keep your heart concealed
Why--Are the days so lonely
Where can a heart go free
And who will dry the tears that no one sees
There must be someone
To share your silent dreams

Chorus
Caught like a leaf in the wind
Lookin' for a friend--Where can you turn
Whisper the words of a prayer—
And you'll find Him there
Arms open wide--Love in His eyes

Jesus--He meets you where you are
Jesus--He heals your secret scars
All the love you're longing for is
Jesus--The friend of a wounded heart
Repeat Chorus

*(Lyrics by Claire Cloninger and Wayne
Watson Used by permission)*

26
HOW ARE YOU *REALLY* FEELING?

When we were in the military, one of my "roles" as a good wife was to attend many officers' wives' gatherings. I remember with much disdain the nauseous feeling I would get when attending these events. Not all, but a few of the wives wore their husband's rank on their sleeves. As if being a Major or Lt. Colonel somehow gave them supremacy over us lower ranking wives. This honestly made me laugh more than it offended me. What did make me sad, however, was feeling like when I would try and talk to women that I saw on a regular basis, their answer to "How are you?" was always, "Fine." Somehow, that answer never did seem quite honest to me.

I have been as plastic as they were many times in my life. To risk being honest with others is very scary, for we don't ever have a guarantee that if we reveal our truest selves that others will like us. Most of my life, I really didn't have a full grasp of how to express my negative feelings in a healthy way. I think the feeling of "gladness" was my favorite default for most of my early life and I would often break into a nervous snicker when I felt fear or anger. Until recovery, I never knew why. One of the greatest gifts I received from attending the Bethesda Workshop in 2007 was that I learned to recognize and honor what I was truly feeling instead of masking it with snickers or a façade of happiness.

Being raised in a "good Christian family," I honestly thought the only feelings I could feel were: sadness for those who were hurting or who were unsaved; anger at the sin in the world and at Satan; and—my family's favorite feeling—gladness. After all, I was a "King's kid!" What more could I want in life? Now, don't get me wrong, I love to feel happy! Recovery work has taught me, though, that a lot of the time that happy feeling has been merely a band-aid sealing my truest emotions. Many times, I have used laughter or pollyanna thinking to deny feelings I didn't want to face or didn't know how to deal with if I did face them.

By the time I married Tom, I was the smiling-est, happiest, people pleasing-est person I knew. I'm not saying that it's wrong to be happy, but a lot of times I wasn't honest to myself or to others when I did have negative feelings and I certainly didn't know how to speak truthfully about them, if I did identify them! So, it's not surprising that when I entered the small group time at the Bethesda Workshop, I soon realized that I had a mountain of anger in me that was buried under a whole lot of happy. This was my coping mechanism because I was scared to death to face my fears, anger, loneliness, hurt, shame, guilt, and sadness.

I was asked at the workshop, "How Do You feel?" I looked down at the list on the floor from Chip Dodd's book, *The Voice of the Heart* and saw the words: *fear, anger, hurt, sad, lonely, guilt, shame* and *glad.* I answered, "I'm glad," yet as I spoke those plastic words, I knew how hypocritical they sounded, in light of the fact that I was at a workshop for spouses whose husbands were sex addicts! Glad? Well, honestly? Not really.

I had no idea until I started allowing myself to *feel* that I was really, really, really angry at Tom for being emotionally and physically unfaithful to me for seventeen years and for not being my "savior!" I was really, really angry at his job that required him to be gone over half of that time leaving me to raise our three girls **alone** without a father figure. Not only was I frustrated at my husband, I was also angry at myself for my own failures, character weaknesses, and flaws.

I was lonely, so lonely all those nights while Tom had been gone with his work, and I was so afraid that he would keep on hurting me. I was also afraid, in my deepest places, that I would not be able to muster the strength and courage to walk out and raise our girls without him.

I was hurt, so hurt that the vow Tom had made to me to love, honor, and cherish our marriage had been broken. I was sad that every dream I had dreamed as a little girl seemed to be marred by the fact that I had either botched the plan myself or that my husband's addiction had affected those dreams.

I felt guilt that my love and affection for my husband had not been enough to persuade Tom to quit looking at porn and that perhaps somehow if only I had been prettier or sexier, maybe this wouldn't have happened.

Of course, now I know that most of those feelings were based on lies that I believed and not on God's truth. As soon as I finally dared to begin peeling back the layers of my unhealthy coping mechanisms and all the denying and minimizing I was so good at doing, I found my tender heart wanting desperately to find healing and wholeness. It was at this juncture in my life that I began to risk feeling again, one moment at a time, not shaming myself for the emotion, just learning to "sit in it." Psalm 46:10 says, "Be still, and know that I am God." To *be still* and allow myself to really feel every emotion in my deepest places was something totally new to me and, honestly, scared me to death. God has taught me the benefit of acknowledging my soul's cry and the discipline of sitting in that emotion for however long it takes to honor it.

One of the many gifts that has come from our recovery has been that I have learned to honor my heart. If I am feeling insecure or afraid of something, I tell Tom as soon as I recognize the feeling so that we can talk about it. If I am feeling lonely, I acknowledge that emotion and ask him to hold my hand or just spend time with me. If I need to ask him an important question, I don't cower in fear. I ask him. I've learned to tell him quickly if I am feeling angry or hurt about something. I have learned to "speak my truth" because I long for intimacy with him. Today, if someone I know asks me how I'm feeling, I can honestly tell them the truth, and sometimes that means I'm not "glad!"

The following chart is from Chip Dodd's, *The Voice of the Heart,* a book that has changed my life and taught me how to honor the God-given emotions I feel every day.

CHIP DODD'S FEELINGS CHART

Taken with permission from The Voice of the Heart
(Emphasis added from what I've learned.)

FEELING:	IMPAIRMENT:
HURT	Resentment
SAD	Self-Pity
LONELY	Apathy – [I just don't care.]
FEAR	Anxiety/Rage
ANGER	Depression/ Perfectionism Resignation
SHAME ["I <u>am</u> bad."]	Toxic Shame/Pride/Rage
GUILT ["I <u>did</u> something bad."]	Inadequacy/Paranoia [Toxic Shame]
GLAD	Entertainment

BENEFIT:

Puts a name to our woundedness and
begins healing as we seek help.

Allows us to value and honor what
we have lost or missed.

Allows us to ask for help and reach
out for intimacy with others.

Can prepare us and increase our faith and wisdom.

Can help us find the truth, and
establish healthy boundaries.

Can awaken us to humility while spurring us
to surrender our toxic shame to Christ.

Gives us the freedom to ask for forgiveness when
we have offended others, even ourselves.

When we are honest with our other seven feelings, this
one reveals the fullness and richness of life. Brings Joy!

What we feel matters. How we respond to those feelings makes the difference between living in a healthy way or not. God has given each of us feelings that are indicators of our heart. I believe that by honoring those feelings, we can live in a better way that is based on honesty and truth not only to ourselves but to others.

Facing Your Hippos This Week:

This week write in your journal each day about what you are feeling, using Chip Dodd's feeling chart. It will feel awkward and even strange at first to dig deep inside and allow yourself to honor the feelings you are feeling. But I promise if you do, you will begin to feel a new sense of freedom in your life. Acknowledge your feelings, "sit in them" for as many minutes, days or hours as you need to, honoring your heart.

As you are honest with your feelings, ask God to show you what you should do about them. If you are feeling *sadness*, ask Jesus if there's something you need to honor by sitting in that feeling for a time. If you are feeling *anger*, ask Jesus what you need to do with that anger. Do you need to speak your truth in love to someone? Do you need to set some boundaries with someone who has crossed over your boundary? Whatever you need to do, seek God's help and he will be faithful to show you what you need to do. If you are feeling *guilt*, ask God to show you areas where you might need to make amends to others you have inadvertently or intentionally offended. Quickly say you're sorry to them and move on!

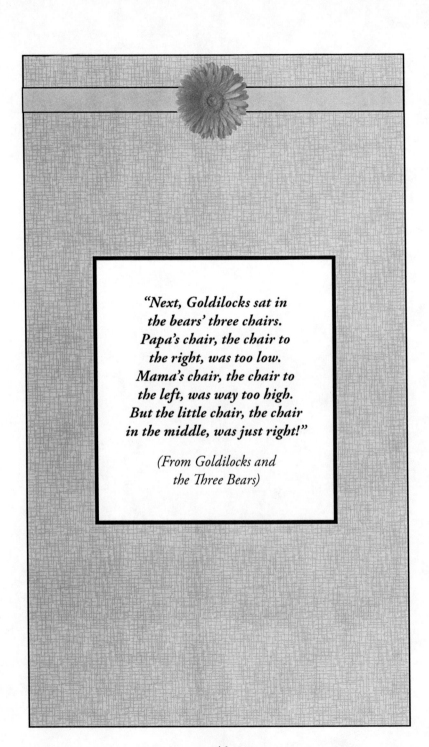

"*Next, Goldilocks sat in the bears' three chairs. Papa's chair, the chair to the right, was too low. Mama's chair, the chair to the left, was way too high. But the little chair, the chair in the middle, was just right!*"

(From Goldilocks and the Three Bears)

27
THE THREE CHAIRS

In the early spring of 2007, my counselor recommended I attend "Healing for Spouses," a weekend seminar from Bethesda Workshops, a counterpart to Tom's "Healing for Sexual Addicts" seminar. One of the greatest lessons I took from that weekend was called "The Three Chairs," a visual developed by internationally recognized psychotherapist, Marilyn Murray. Seeing this helped me to understand better the constant battle my mind and heart had been waging for most of my teen and adult life.

Our seminar leader stood in front of about 40 of us ladies, from teenagers to adults. She placed three chairs in the front, all in a row. She pointed to the first chair to her right. In it sat a sweet little teddy bear. The name of this bear was Wounded Child, or a child who had been wounded by the trauma of abuse or abandonment. This child was dominant or present when the person chose to live in the past, reliving their abuses and trauma, instead of walking in the newness of life.

When I was a child, I talked like a child, I thought like a child, I reasoned like a child. When I became a man, I put childish ways behind me. (1 Corinthians 13:11)

Next, she pointed to the chair on her left, which held a big, stuffed gorilla. The gorilla's name was Survivor Child, or a child who coped with her woundedness in a variety of unhealthy ways. This child would become dominant or present when the person chose passive-aggressive behavior, angry outbursts, or unreasonable control to solve problems, instead of walking in the newness of life.

I know that nothing good lives in me, that is, in my sinful nature.
For I have the desire to do what is good, but I cannot carry it out.
For what I do is not the good I want to do; no, the evil I do not want
to do—this I keep on doing. Now if I do what I do not want to do,
it is no longer I who do it, but it is sin living in me that does it.
(Romans 7:18-20)

Last, the seminar leader pointed to the middle chair, which was empty. This represented the God Child that all of us long to be—the original child, created by God, feeling her feelings freely, comfortable in her own skin. The God Child is a mature, healthy person who handles life's storms in a healthy manner and who knows how to take care of her physical, emotional, and spiritual well-being. She can speak truthfully to others and knows her own heart better than anyone else's. She is neither needy nor angry. The God Child, who sits in the middle chair, is at peace with her world, accepting her limitations and imperfections, not blaming anyone for her circumstances.

You were taught with regard to your former way of life, to put off
your old self, which is being corrupted by its deceitful desires; to be
made new in the attitude of your minds; and to put on the new
self, created to be like God in true righteousness and holiness.
(Ephesians 4:22)

The lesson that I reaped from this demonstration was this: As a wife of a sex addict, I first and foremost need to learn to take care of myself. When we left Minnesota, I was depressed, overweight, and spent most of my days walking around in a brain fog. Yet, I didn't have the emotional, spiritual, or physical strength to seek help for myself. I allowed my circumstances and taking care of my family to consume me. *I had lost myself.* I was enmeshed in Tom's addiction and allowed my own life to lose its focus and purpose.

So, both Tom and I began to listen to our hearts, address our feelings, and to communicate with each other in a whole new and exciting way. We learned to sit in the middle (God Child) chair, instead of defaulting to childish patterns (Wounded Child) or using unhealthy coping mechanisms (Survivor Child). I learned to take better care of myself spiritually, emotionally, and physically, taking responsibility for what was mine, instead of blaming others for all of my problems. Tom began the long process of learning how to share his feelings without hiding in shame and without medicating the pain (Survivor Child). He began to learn to honor his feelings by calling a sponsor from S-A, instead of looking to the false intimacy of pornography as a pain reliever.

Three Chairs Chart

The following chart is a visual that God has given me to help me better understand my true feelings and actions. From the exercise at the Bethesda Workshop, I saw, for the first time in my life, this idea of three chairs. Over the past several years in recovery and working with Safe Haven, I have developed this visual of three chairs and have listed some of the unhealthy and healthy characteristics that might accompany each position.

This visual has revolutionized my life. On days when I am feeling particularly "childish," I have learned to be more aware of this and when I recognize my behavior, I see myself in the baby chair. I ask myself if that is really where I want to spend my day. The answer is usually "NO" and I choose to move myself over to the middle, healthy chair where I can be the healthy adult I want to be.

Some days, I have been known to become extremely angry when my expectations aren't met. I have been known to become silent (and deadly) and withhold my true feelings from those closest to me who are trying to talk to me. I have learned to recognize this unhealthy behavior and see myself in the coping chair. As soon as I own these unhealthy behaviors, I choose to move myself over to the middle, healthy chair where I can speak my truth and surrender my unrealistic expectations to One who is more than able to meet my every need.

I pray this visual helps you in your daily walk.

The Three Chairs

Which Chair Are You In?

Wounded Child	Healthy Adult	Survivor/Coping
Toxic Shame Insecure Believing I am not enough I don't matter Afraid Spinning In the Fog Impatient Pouting Reacting to others Needing to put my big girl britches on!	Proactive Speaking my Truth Boundaries Owning my stuff Making Amends Trusting Showing Up Content Surrendered heart, mind & soul Reverent fear of God's sovereignty in my life At Peace Comfy in my own skin.	Passive Aggressive Rage Acting Out Not owning my feelings Not speaking my truth Pollyanna attitude while denying true feelings Blaming others Denial Minimizing Silent Fight or Flight Queen People Pleasers to a fault Performance Based Pleasers

Facing Your Hippos This Week:

Think about it: the next time you are feeling imbalanced in your emotional, physical or spiritual realms, ask yourself, "Okay, which chair am I choosing to sit in right now?" Many days, I am in the baby chair with the pacifier in my mouth, acting like the little girl who didn't get some need met way back in elementary school. When I acknowledge that I am not in the Middle/Healthy Chair that is the beginning of recovery! By seeing the hippo in my life, I then ask myself, "What do I need right now to get me from feeling wounded so that I can move over to the middle chair?" If I can meet my need myself, I do so. If not, I ask the Lord to show me what it is I need to do. Sometimes, I am just lonely and I need to call a friend and just connect with someone. Nine times out of ten, if I will take the time and listen to my heart and hear what it is saying I need, I will then be sitting in that middle chair in no time. And, that's *exactly* where I want to be!

"It is estimated that 90 percent of all physical problems have psychological roots. A growing body of evidence indicates that virtually every ill that can befall the body – from acne to arthritis, headaches to heart disease, cold sores to cancer – is influenced, for better or worse, by our emotions."

(Quoted from *The Complete Guide To Your Emotions And Your Health* p. 563 by Emrika Padus and the editors of *Prevention* magazine in the book, *"Feelings Buried Alive Never Die"* by Karol K. Truman.)

28
OUT ON A LIMB

I'm going to go out on a limb here and share something that I believe may be an unscientific possibility. When I was not emotionally healthy and Tom was in his addiction, I suffered from many stomach and lower abdominal problems. At different times in our marriage, I was diagnosed with irritable bowel syndrome, acid reflux, heartburn (heartache?), endometriosis, ovarian cysts and my colon area hurt almost all of the time. What's interesting to me is that I've met many wives in the similar situation in their marriage who also suffer from similar dis-eases of their body, not to mention mental fog and feeling crazy.

By nature, I used to be a great minimizer and denied the hippos of my life. That's my default, which I fight against every day, but it explains why I put up with my husband's porn addiction for seventeen years of our marriage before threatening to kick him out if he didn't seek help. Instead of honoring my God-given feelings like anger (at the ongoing porn addiction), sadness (at the reality of my marriage and my lack of backbone), hurt (from the infidelity), guilt (from overspending when I didn't have the money to spend), loneliness (because of Tom's job requirements and the emptiness I felt even when we were together) and shame (from the hypocrisy I felt in our marriage), I *stuffed* all these feelings and pretended the hippo was not in the room.

When Tom hit "bottom" and finally began seeking help for his addiction after seventeen years of our marriage, I remember glaring at him across the fellowship hall of our church and hating every last fiber of his being. What I had longed for for so long was finally coming to fruition but the irony was that all of those emotions that had been suppressed inside of me and not honored suddenly began to bubble up within me. It was like trying to tack down a bedroom flat sheet over the hole of a volcano. No amount of clothespins was going to keep the eruption from occurring. In fact, in my thesaurus, do you know that under the word "eruption" is the synonym "disease?" Feelings buried for so long, not honored, not allowed to come out into the Light, will cause the body to feel dis-eased and eventually, those feelings, I believe, will erupt.

On a Sunday in September, the day before our seventeenth wedding anniversary (whoopee!), I woke up feeling "off" but went to church anyway. I led music and told everyone to sing extra loud 'cause I wasn't up to speed. That night, I started getting sick and instead of feeling better after each upchuck, I felt worse. By four in the morning, Tom got in from a trip and I was sicker than I think I had ever been. He took me to the hospital and by the time we arrived in the emergency room, I was almost passed out, lying sideways in the wheelchair.

After taking my vitals and doing an MRI, they deduced I was having some kind of gastric issue because they couldn't "find" my appendix. They hooked me up to an IV and began a morphine drip. After twenty-four hours, I was starting to feel something deep in my soul that told me things were not right. So, I mustered up the strength and all the courage I could find and I asked to see my doctor. He came in and I asked him, "Okay, so I'm not a doctor, but isn't morphine supposed to kill any and *all* pain?" He said, "Yes." Well, at that point, I could still feel a whole lot of pain and honestly, I felt like my body was a helium balloon that was filling up with a trough full of slop! My heart and my brain knew I was going down and fast!

After further conversation with the doctor who at first insisted that it was just a "gas" issue and some tears on my part, he finally conceded to doing another MRI to double check. They wheeled me down and low and behold, there it was: in the lower right quadrant of my abdomen was my very low appendix that had ruptured. Within twenty minutes, I was in the operating room and out like a light. They found my "abnormally low" appendix and removed all of the pieces, putting me on a super antibiotic that supposedly flushed out my system and any living bacteria from here to kingdom come. After five days in the hospital, I came home and spent the next six weeks trying to learn how to breathe again and mourning the loss of my bikini figure. (Okay, I never had a bikini figure, but I can dream, can't I?)

I will never know this for sure, but I cannot help but wonder if the reason my appendix was so low was in part due to my denying my feelings. Now that I know the freedom that comes from honoring what I feel and the joy that comes with releasing them to a higher power that is more than able to handle my circumstances, I no longer have irritable bowel syndrome or any ulcerative symptoms. Some people might sneer at this unscientific speculation—I don't. I know how I used to feel—all bound up and not free—and I know how I feel now.

I really believe that we are holistic beings created with an emotional, spiritual, and physical component. Like the trinity, we are three separate but interrelated parts. I also believe that when we do not deal with our feelings in a healthy way and resort to unhealthy coping mechanisms of the Survival Child/Coping Chair or the unproductive and stagnant frame of mind of the Wounded Child/Baby Chair, it can have an adverse affect on our overall well-being and can manifest itself in our physical realm. Remember the visual in the last chapter of the three chairs: the middle one is the healthy one. The left one is the baby chair and the right one is the coping chair. The goal is to be in the middle chair as much as possible and to live out of its characteristics. Remember, the Bible says we are created in the image of God and that our bodies are the temple of the Holy Spirit. It just makes sense to me that we need to honor our feelings, keeping our emotional, physical, and, ultimately, our spiritual parts in balance.

It is with great trepidation that I have written this chapter as I know what I am saying is purely speculation and not scientific. I am not suggesting that if you acknowledge your feelings your medical problems will magically disappear! What I am suggesting is that our bodies let us know when there is something imbalanced. I think dis-ease of the body and pain are two great indicators of this possible truth.

Part of recovery for me has been to learn how to be more aware of my physical body and its relationship to the emotional and spiritual part of who I am. In her book, "Feelings Buried Alive Never Die," Karol K. Truman lists common dis-eases of the body that she believes are the result of feelings that have not been honored or dealt with in a healthy way. Though I don't agree with everything in her book, I do agree with her theory that feelings buried alive really never do die. One way or another, they will manifest themselves. I believe this because I have experienced exactly what she talks about in her book. I have seen it played out in my own life and in the lives of many other women.

Facing Your Hippos This Week:

This week, I want you to be more aware of any areas in your physical body where you may have dis-ease or dis-comfort. Don't minimize and don't deny them. If you want, get Karol K. Truman's book, "Feelings Buried Alive Never Die" and read over the list in the back of her book and see if your dis-ease or dis-comfort matches up to the feelings that you may have been denying.

Remember: God has created you in His image. You are His masterpiece and treasure. Recovery helps us to begin to see just how beautiful we truly are and helps us to know **we are worth it!**

Some time later, Jesus went up to Jerusalem for a feast of the Jews. Now there is in Jerusalem near the Sheep Gate a pool, which in Aramaic is called Bethesda and which is surrounded by five covered colonnades. Here a great number of disabled people used to lie – the blind, the lame, the paralyzed. One who was there had been an invalid for thirty-eight years. When Jesus saw him lying there and learned that he had been in this condition for a long time, he asked him, "Do you want to get well?"

(John 5:1-6)

29

DO YOU *WANT* TO BE WELL?

I'll never forget the day Tom and I got married. The day started out overcast and promising showers. By the time the wedding party was assembled in the dressing rooms preparing for the big event, the clouds had formed in military procession directly overhead and the floodgates opened.

I felt sad and thought, "If the rain doesn't stop, no one will come." One of my wiser, older (probably about the age I am right now!) friends spoke some sage wisdom to my young heart. She said, "People do what they want to do. If they want to be here to celebrate your wedding day, then they will come no matter what." And, you know, she was right. People came, shook off the heavy raindrops, found their way to their seats, and celebrated with us. My aunts and uncles came all the way from Illinois. Those who didn't want to come, well, they didn't come and it wouldn't have mattered if the skies had been sunny. They would have done what they wanted to do.

Last night my youngest daughter and I were the only ones home. We had dinner together on the front porch overlooking the landscape of the valley we live in, enjoying the cool fall weather. After eating, I meandered down the sidewalk, checking over my poor plants that looked a bit deprived of water or fertilizer.

Looking closer, I discovered one of those creepy "zipper" spiders on one of them. I called my daughter over to check it out and she had the sudden and "great idea" to get a mason jar and catch it! Why I immediately went in the house and got a jar to do just that, I'll never know. So, we caught it in the jar and quickly and firmly sealed the top. We brought the spider in and admired its spindly legs and freakish form.

The next morning, Mr. Spidee, as we named him, sat on the counter awaiting my daughter, Vic, to take him to school to show her biology teacher. As the flurry of early risers in our home came and went, and after wishing them a safe journey to school, I walked back inside. There, to my dismay, I saw our friend *still* on the counter. I quickly texted Vic and asked her what she wanted me to do. She informed me to "Let him go, Mom. I feel sorry for him. Don't you think we should let him go?" With a smile on my face, I shook my head, realizing how caring her words were for this creepy, gnarly spider. So, like all of us who aspire to be good moms, I picked up the mason jar and walked outside and opened the lid and tried and tried to jiggle the spider loose from its hold on the bottom of the jar. He wouldn't budge. I thought to myself, "Silly spider. He doesn't get it that the top's off and he can go if he wants to." I ended up leaving the jar upside down, teetering off the edge of the deck in hopes that the spider would figure out his happy, new situation.

As I texted Vic back, I said, "Silly spider. He doesn't realize he is free yet." As I typed those words, the Lord spoke to me. He said, "That's just like you sometimes. You are free to trust and live in complete abandonment to my will for your life—not bound up with all the things that hold you down—but you don't get it that you are free." Just like being labeled a codependent by counselors alongside my husband's addiction, I can choose freedom or I can choose prison.

This is true. I know it full well in the deepest places of my heart. I've seen it in my own life when I choose to cling to the past, hurt, and pain while God is standing at my heart's door. I hear Him asking me, "Do you *want* to be free?" Like the spider that doesn't "get it" that he is free, I am prone to cling to temporal things that do not satisfy. See, I do what I want to do in this life. I can say all day long that I want to be free, but if I don't reach up and grab it and live out what I know to be true, then I'm as stuck as that spider was in the jar—waiting, hoping things will change. While, all the while, God has already opened up the way for me to be free if I'll just trust him fully.

The interesting reality of this life is that God gives us the option to either trust Him one hundred percent or to live a life of paralysis. No amount of nagging, pleading, or begging can coerce my husband to live as a godly man and to honor his vows to me. On the other hand, no amount of Bible study, Scripture memorization, or counseling can force me to fall on my knees and surrender my life to the Father's will. We both must choose to either be well or to stay in our crippled conditions.

In John 5:6, Jesus asked the cripple, "Do you want to get well?" See, here was the Lord of all creation offering the man a way out of his circumstance. All he had to do was take the hand that was being extended to him and live! In John 5:6-7, the man rambles on about his hard life and to Jesus that no one would help him. Jesus then turns this complaining and blaming on its ear and commands him to "Get Up! Pick up your mat and walk!" (Do you wonder if Jesus was thinking, "Get over yourself, Buddy, and quit your complaining!")

I can't help but know that Jesus has felt the same way about me at times. Grumbling, complaining, making excuses and blaming: I've used them all as a means of avoiding the truest questions. God has taught me through this journey that I can be healthy emotionally, spiritually, and physically if I will just *choose* him and his way. I heard someone say one time, "Unless the pain of staying the same becomes greater than the pain of change, we will not change." So to change my life requires a choice on my part. Do I *want* to be well – to do whatever I can in the midst of my circumstance or do I want to stay where I am? The choice really is up to me.

Facing Your Hippos This Week:

How about you? Do you ever catch yourself feeling sorry for yourself and choose to sit on your mat of doubt, fear, complacency, self-pity, or shame? I know I have done all of those things at different times. There's good news! You can *choose* to be well and to walk in the freedom that Christ gives!

This week:

> 1. Ask the Lord to help you see when you are living as a cripple and then *choose* to get up and walk out of that situation!
>
> 2. Go to the Word and in the concordance, look up the word "TRUST." Write down every verse that speaks to your heart about trusting God and meditate on those verses each day this week. Be encouraged!
>
> 3. Every time you catch yourself going back to your old ways of living like the invalid at the pool, recite a verse about trusting God. By replacing the old, negative thoughts and beliefs in your mind, you will begin to be transformed. Remember Jesus said, "Do you *want* to be well?" The choice is up to you whether you live a crippled life or walk in the abundance that only Christ can bring!

For your Maker is your husband—the Lord Almighty is his name —the Holy One of Israel is your Redeemer; he is called the God of all the earth.

(Isaiah 54:5)

30
GOD'S TRUTH FOR ME

The mind is a powerful thing. Satan preys on us, "looking for someone to devour." (1 Peter 5:8) He is a master of deceit trying to trip us up if we are not careful and diligent in our daily pursuit of God. Over the years in my walk with Christ, God has taught me the incredible importance of knowing him and of understanding his many attributes. I can stand on the foundation of God's truth and *not falter*.

I have done a lot of soul searching over the last six years and will continue to do so until I die. Being in recovery from any stronghold or addiction in our life is a lifelong process, a lifestyle. Part of my "work" has been to understand why I allowed myself to live with a man who I knew was being emotionally unfaithful to me. I mean, fool me once, shame on you. Fool me twice, shame on me! I have come to know that part of the reason why I put up with Tom's behavior was that I didn't have the courage to raise our daughters on my own. That may sound cowardly and shallow, I know, but it's the truth. I think a lot of wives stay in a similar situation for the same reason.

The sad thing is that I had heard and memorized Scripture all of my life, had been in thousands of church settings, had read lots of Christian books, and yet, I didn't believe God to be *El Shaddai*, the All-Sufficient and Almighty One, capable of setting me free from my situation. It wasn't until I read the book, *Lord, I Want to Know You* by Kay Arthur, that I got my first taste of the myriad of names of the sufficient God in the Bible. Her book showed me, for the first time in my life, just how perfect, steadfast and trustworthy my God is. He is our provider, *Jehovah-Jireh*, our healer, *Jehovah-Rapha*, and our banner, *Jehovah Nissi*. He sees us, *El-Roi*, is Almighty, *El-Shaddai*, our Lord, *Adonai,* and is our shepherd, *Jehovah-Raah*. Basically, in a nutshell: God is enough. I really believe that Tom's sexual addiction is the impetus that God used to help me to get on my knees and find Him in a way I would have never found Him otherwise. I know Christ now. I trust God now more than I have ever trusted anyone else on this earth and my foundation is now solidly built on the eternal truth that He is mine and I am His. Nothing can separate me from that—nothing!

God has taught me that when I feel afraid, I must stop and make a choice: Do I believe the lies I'm hearing in my head that say, "You don't matter" or "you are defective" or "you're not good enough," and on and on. Or do I choose at that moment to trust God's truth that says:

Ps. 139:14 - I praise you because I am fearfully and wonderfully made; your works are wonderful, I know that full well.

Ps. 45:11 - The king is *enthralled* by your beauty; honor him for he is your LORD.

Philippians 4:6-7 - Do not be anxious about anything, but in everything, by prayer and petition, with thanksgiving, present your requests to God. And the peace of God, which transcends all understanding, will guard your hearts and your minds in Christ Jesus.

Philippians 4:19 - And my God will meet all your needs according to his glorious riches in Christ Jesus.

Ephesians 3:20 - Now to him who is able to do immeasurably more than all we ask or imagine. (God, our Father, my heavenly husband, is able to do for my life and my husband's life more than I can even begin to dream. That's an amazing promise to me!)

In 2004, God revealed to me a truth about himself that literally changed my way of thinking. It was one of the many things God used to encourage my heart to seek healing. In her book, *The Confident Woman*, Anabel Gilham paraphrased the Scripture:

> *For your Maker is your husband, the LORD Almighty is his name. He is the Redeemer and the Holy One of Israel. The God of the whole earth is His name.*
>
> *(Isaiah 54:5)*

As I read those words, they pierced my heart and, for the first time, I realized that all the loneliness, pain, and betrayal caused by my earthly husband's addiction did not change the fact that my heavenly husband loved me. The God of the universe, the Creator, *Elohim*, was saying to me, "**I** am your husband and **I am enough.**

There's something so very beautiful about knowing that there is an Almighty God that is above all names, people, and things who actually takes the time to genuinely and fervently care for each of us. That reliable affection supersedes all of life's disappointments and hurts and lifts us up to a place that is victorious. Knowing that we are loved unconditionally and, best of all, that we will never be betrayed by God, gives me the courage to love again, because my deepest needs are being met in him. He is unchangeable and trustworthy.

I am loved. You are loved. We are free to love others even when there is a great chance they'll let us down; and, honestly, there's a great chance we may let them down as well. We can be secure in

Christ, knowing our self worth is found in some ONE that cannot and will not leave us nor forsake us. It is because Jesus has done so much for us that we can *risk* loving others. God's love is more than able to heal even the deepest hurts and wounds of our lives, filling up the empty places, and renewing us.

The question for me each day and each moment is this: Do I believe God? Do I believe His Word and do I *trust* that he means what he says? Do I have the faith, even the courage, to have confidence in the One who will never leave or forsake me? Am I willing to push aside the onslaught of lies Satan tempts me to believe and cling to God's truth minute by minute, day by day? Regardless of whether or not our spouses and friends respond to our needs, we can choose to stand on God's uncompromising, unfailing truth.

Looking back now, over my life, I can see how much I lived each day as a wounded "victim." For years, I blamed Tom for all the ills in our marriage, instead of trusting God to be sufficient enough to meet my needs. God has shown me the beauty and power of his love letter to me, the Bible. I have found my greatest joys and victories in its pages. In it, I've found peace, true peace that truly satisfies my greatest needs. I've learned to recognize, unveil, and stand up to the hippos in my life, ushering them out of their dominant places in my heart by trusting God and his sufficiency.

Facing Your Hippos This Week:

When we lived in Arkansas, I had a friend who shared a book with me that has been a great source of strength and encouragement. It is Kay Arthur's book, *"Lord, I Want to Know You."* I encourage you to purchase it and begin reading and learning about the different names of God and his many character qualities. They are available to you and to me each and every moment. As you come to understand Him as your Provider, *Jehovah-Jireh,* I hope you will begin to thank him in those moments when you see him providing for you whether it is in a word of encouragement from a friend who calls or by providing monetary needs at just the right time. As you come to know him as your healer, *Jehovah-Rapha,* I hope you will immediately praise him in the moments of your healing, whether it is in the physical, emotional, or spiritual realm. He is with you and he loves you more than you can ever begin to imagine. Bask in his love this week and be transformed!

Very early in the morning, while it was still dark, Jesus got up, left the house and went off to a solitary place, where he prayed.

(Mark 1:35)

****

I believe each time we say "Our Father," God looks at His hands, where He has carved us. ("I have carved you in the palm of my hand." See Isaiah 49:16.) He looks at His hands, and He sees us there. How wonderful the tenderness and love of God!

(From No Greater Love, Mother Teresa)

31
PRAYER AND TIME IN THE WORD

The greatest gift I give not only to myself but also to my family is to spend the first part of each day praying and studying God's Word. There is nothing more important or more empowering. Prayer is a constant communication with my Creator and the lover of my soul that I don't want to live without. God's truths from the Bible are *life* to me and literally fill up the empty places in my soul, giving me power and ammunition to walk victoriously each day. I am thankful that I've learned these truths and hope that if you, the reader, have not made spending time and prayer with God a priority, that you will begin to do so today. It's never too late to start and the benefits are amazing!

One of my favorite Christian heroes is Mother Teresa. I've always admired her life and work. Hers was a life poured out for the cause of Christ. She wasn't a glory seeker, but a God seeker, willing to care for the lowest of the low of Calcutta, India. In her book, *No Greater Love,* she talks about the importance of prayer.

> Does your mind and your heart go to Jesus as soon as you get up in the morning? This is prayer, that you turn your mind and heart to God. Prayer is the very life of oneness, of being one with Christ. Therefore, prayer is as necessary as the air, as the blood in our body, as anything, to keep us

alive to the grace of God. We must pray perseveringly and with great love. If we don't pray, our presence will have no power, our words will have no power.

I want my life to matter for the cause of Christ and God has taught me that without prayer and the power found within it, I can do *nothing*. In 1 Thessalonians 5:17 in the King James Version, it states, "Pray without ceasing." It is a dialog, really, with our Creator, a continual conversation where no one hangs up.

When I'm driving behind an obnoxiously slow driver, I pray not only that they will hurry up, but also for my own (ugly) attitude toward the person. Now, please, please don't think I've got it all together and just by praying I don't ever experience road rage! On the contrary, my friends! I struggle sometimes with wanting to run people off the road, but the difference in how I used to be before learning to pray without ceasing and now is that I *recognize* my road rage and immediately ask God to help me slow down and be more compassionate, more *patient*.

Let me share a good illustration of how God has helped me learn this. In years past, I used to suddenly become Mario Andretti at the wheel if someone dared to poke along in front of me. "Drive the speed limit at least, Buddy!" Well, the good Lord gave me three daughters who have now all gone through driver's education courses. Part of that process has been that I have had to learn to sit *patiently* in the passenger's seat as they have learned the skill of driving – slower than the speed limit at times – on busy roads. Ah, now I get it, Lord. That realization has softened my heart toward slow drivers and by praying for them and asking God to give me *compassion*, well, I'm better about road rage than I've ever been.

In addition to praying without ceasing, God has taught me the treasure of His Word. For years, I would make excuses and feel ashamed that I couldn't memorize Scripture passages. I didn't let that stop me from reading the Bible. I thought that at least maybe something would stick and it was better to read than not to read, so I read. And do you know what? God has taught me that when I need to recall a Scripture, He will supply what I need to say at that moment! It has happened to me time after time. I have learned it's more important to seek God and his truths to me rather than to pressure myself into some legalistic mantra like, "If I don't quote large chunks of Scripture I'm not a true Christian." Humbug! I'm basking in spending time with my Lord and in those moments, He fills me up to overflowing with the promises, hope, and encouragement that come from reading his Word.

Praying continually to One who is more than able to meet our daily needs and seeking God first by reading his Word daily are two vital truths that will transform our spiritual life. It's not a legalistic set of rules that says, "If I miss a day of reading my Bible, I'm going to hell," or "If I forget to pray, God won't love me." No! It's about seeking God, first with all of our heart, mind, and soul and being intentional about our spiritual growth. Remember, the bottom line is this: God loves you and created you for relationship with him. The only way to get to know him better is to spend time with him.

Facing Your Hippos This Week:

One of my favorite Bible disciplines is to read in Psalms and Proverbs every day. These books are rich in wisdom and personal growth applications. I use the calendar date to decide which book in Psalms I want to read and add "30" to that number until I've exhausted the book. For Proverbs, I simply read whatever chapter correlates with the date on the calendar. For example: If it's the eighth day, I read Psalms 8, 38, 68, 98, 128, and Proverbs 8.

I encourage you to begin reading these two books of the Bible as often as you can. Start your day by spending time with God in prayer and meditating on His Word. It will change your day for the better!

*May the God of hope fill you
with all joy and peace as you trust in him,
so that you may overflow with hope
by the power of the Holy Spirit.*

(Romans 15:13)

****

*I pray that out of his glorious riches he
may strengthen you with power through
his Spirit in your inner being, so that
Christ may dwell in your hearts through
faith. And I pray that you, being rooted
and established in love, may have power,
together with all the saints, to grasp how
wide and long and high and deep is the
love of Christ, and to know this love that
surpasses knowledge – that you may be filled
to the measure of all the fullness of God.*

(Ephesians 3:16-19)

32
THE EMPTY PLACES

I saw a visual one time about learning how to fill up the empty places in our lives with things of eternal significance. I have never forgotten it and have used it several times over the years in various settings. The idea uses a tall, glass flower vase. The second part of the demonstration uses ordinary rice. It represents all of the possible ways I might fill my day. Some of the possibilities in my normal twenty-four hour period include: making my daughter's breakfast and lunches, feeding our horse, goats, bunny, two chickens, collie dog and two cats, calling friends to check in and up with them, doing an exercise DVD, going shopping, running errands, cleaning the house, doing laundry, baking a cake, decorating a cake, checking my emails, recording my daily receipts into Quicken, well, you get the idea. Though all of these things are not negative in any sense of the word, they can take up my entire day, leaving no room for spiritual growth if I let them. The third part of the visual includes walnuts. They represent reading my Bible, prayer, seeking the Holy Spirit's power in my life and meditating on the Word.

So, with the "rice," I fill up the vase with those things that require my attention or at least seem to. The jar usually fills up to the very top and all of a sudden, I realize that there's not any room for the "walnuts" of spiritual nourishment in my day. This is a perplexing problem that at times in the past in my spiritual journey has left me feeling quite sad, guilty and well, empty. I long to sit in the middle chair, making good choices that nurture and feed my whole being and spending time with God is crucial to my well-being.

So, in the visual, I dump out the rice and start again. Just like God doesn't give up on me, He allows second chances. Taking the vase the second time, I begin first with the "Walnuts" of spiritual priority in my day. Around that most important treasure, I fill in the "Rice" of commitments and tyrannies of the present that are inevitably part of my day. Amazingly, the rice and walnuts fit perfectly into the vase. This time, my day is different because I have made the choice to make the time to seek God's agenda for my day and have allowed Him to fill up the empty places in me that only He can fill.

Once, I heard Beth Moore say, "Only Jesus and His Holy Spirit who lives in me can fill me up completely." That is life-changing to me. Each day, I ask the LORD to fill up my empty places whenever I feel overwhelmed, scared, lonely, or insecure. I do this as often and as early in my day as I can. I want to carpe diem (Seize the Day!) and know that He promises if we ask, we will receive.

 Facing Your Hippos This Week:

Make a copy of the prayer below on a pretty colored piece of paper and place it in a prominent place. Make it a point to read it each morning, meditating on the truth that Jesus alone is sufficient to meet all of your needs and to fill up any empty places in you.

"Lord, Jesus, thank you for this day that You have made. Please fill up every empty place in me that only YOU can fill with your precious 'Living Water,' —your Holy Spirit. Fill me up so completely that from the overflow of who you are, I will be able to 'show up' in the lives of others this day."

For what the law was powerless to do in that it was weakened by the sinful nature, God did by sending his own Son in the likeness of sinful man to be a sin offering. And so he condemned sin in sinful man, in order that the righteous requirements of the law might be fully met in us, who do not live according to the sinful nature but according to the Spirit.

(Romans 8:3-4)

33
POWERLESSNESS

The most important truth I pray you will take with you after reading this book is that we cannot, we *cannot*, control what others do. We truly are "powerless" over our spouse's addictions and over the dependencies with which we ourselves struggle. Admitting our powerlessness paradoxically opens the door to more power, strength, and healing in our own lives.

In the Serenity Bible: A Companion for Twelve Step Recovery, Step 1 says, "We admitted we were powerless over our dependencies – that our lives had become unmanageable." When I first heard the word "powerless" I wasn't exactly sure what it meant. Was it saying I was weak, incapable or paralyzed as my thesaurus stated? If it did, I certainly didn't want any part of that!

My recovery Bible also says, "The addiction cycle, as a rule, cannot be broken without yielding to a Power outside ourselves. We may have to surrender again and again, as we admit our powerlessness over, not only the primary addiction, but over various other aspects of our lives. We must recognize when we are powerless over people, places and situations and learn to let those things go."

As a recovering codependent, I have had to learn to admit that I am powerless over my fears, my wanting to control others and my desire to run if things get too hard. By admitting my weaknesses and surrendering them over to God, I have learned to "do less – to yield, to surrender, to let go." (Serenity Bible, page 23)

After Tom sought sobriety on his own, I began releasing myself from the false responsibility of being the detective in our marriage. By admitting I was powerless over his addictions, it freed me to focus on my own shortcomings and begin to grow as a person. Instead of feeling like I was weak for admitting my human frailties, I began to see myself as God does: in need of His power. Instead of allowing my pride to keep me from seeking help, I began to ask for help from others who cared for me and found the freedom that comes from being honest with my situation.

The second step in understanding just how powerless we are comes when we acknowledge God's sufficiency in handling whatever we are powerless over. Step Two says we "Came to believe that a Power greater than ourselves could restore us to sanity." We have to believe there is something or someone greater than the addictions and dependencies that have bound us up and had their hold over us. It's really about seeing ourselves as people in need of a Savior and realizing we don't have it all together like we'd like the world to believe.

Lastly, Step Three says we "Made a decision to turn our will and our lives over to the care of God as we understood Him." I love this step because it requires faith and a willingness on our part to trust God more than our circumstance in order for change to take place.

There's a cost to wholeness. It doesn't just "happen." When I am willing to admit my powerlessness over my own dependencies and my husband's addictions, I am then able to surrender to God's sufficient power.

I am powerless. He is POWERFUL.

 ## Facing Your Hippos This Week:

What is it that you struggle with? Is it fear? Do you obsess over things? Do you feel out of control? Is it anger? What is it in you that you need to admit you are powerless over?

October 9, 2012

Dear Friends,

We dropped by your church today but missed you. We wanted to give you this free resource for your church's library. We represent a non-profit, Safe Haven 4 Women, Inc. Our vision is to offer hope and healing to women who have been adversely affected by the issue of pornography and addictions. This book is 1 of 100 new books that has been selected to be featured at the upcoming Women of Faith Conference in Kansas City, MO on November 2nd and 3rd.

If you have any questions, please feel free to call us. We pray this book will be a source of encouragement and hope for women in your congregation who may be in this difficult situation.

To God be the glory.

Safe Haven 4 Women, Inc.
safehaven4women@gmail.com
615-260-5976

Take a minute right now and write down areas of your life that you have no control over. My list includes: fear of abandonment, road rage, overspending and eating too many mashed potatoes. I am powerless over these things!

After you have spent some time being honest with yourself and God, read your list out loud. Now that you have "Owned your stuff," do you believe that God is able to restore you to sanity? If so, now is the time to surrender whatever you feel you are powerless over to the Lord. He is waiting and is more than able to handle what you are facing this day!

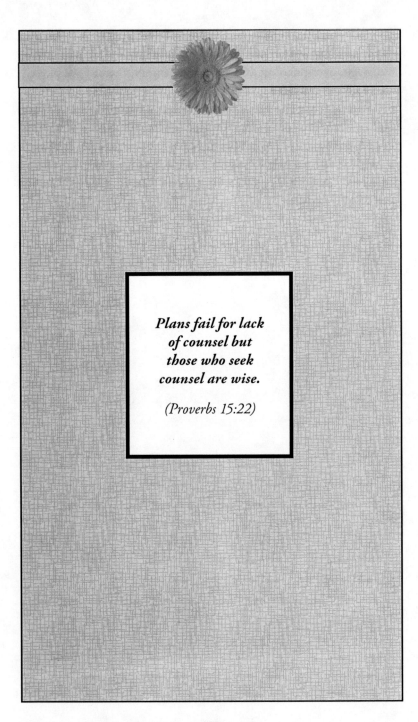

*Plans fail for lack
of counsel but
those who seek
counsel are wise.*

(Proverbs 15:22)

34
IN TIMES OF RELAPSE

Years ago when we lived in North Carolina, I wrote a song entitled, "In His Time." It was my first attempt at penning a song, but strangely enough it has "stuck" throughout the last twenty plus years. The words are simple:

> In His time,
> All things are beautiful
> In His time,
> All things are right
> When we stop looking
> And start listening,
> The hurting stops,
> The healing starts
> And we see that all things come
> In His time.

I have longed for things to just "be all right." The agony of dealing with hard things, whether a mile-high load of laundry or patiently waiting on the Lord to work in Tom's heart and end his addiction after seventeen years, is not on my list of fun things to do. Yet, courage, faith, and wholeness are three characteristics that God has most refined within me as a result of being married to an addict over the years and as a result of coming face to face with my own unhealthy coping mechanisms.

It has been a tremendous struggle for Tom as he has fought the battle of sobriety with both victories and losses. I, too, have battled my own codependent tendencies. Yet, through God's sovereign design for our lives and his unconditional love for us, he has used both of our struggles with addiction and codependency to build us more into his likeness. Truly, what Satan meant for harm, God has turned to good. Through the pain of our sin, God has transformed our lives and has taught us to love him more fully.

The road we are on, the journey we have embarked upon has not been easy and, honestly, I never signed up for this. Somehow, though, God continues to refine both of us as we are learning to trust Him fully. I wish I could say that if you work on your quiet time with God and your husband goes to a support group, his addiction to pornography will just disappear. Oh, how I wish it was that easy. It's not. Living with someone who has an addiction to pornography is like living with someone who has an alcohol problem or a drug problem or a codependency problem. Ultimately, it boils down to their heart and whether or not they *want* to be healthy or not. No amount of nagging or complaining can change a heart. The addict has to want to change and then begin making daily strides to do so. And, that, my friend, is a daily process with victories and losses.

Tom remained sober for three and one-half years as a result of attending an intensive recovery workshop, using a personal therapist who specializes in sex addiction, and after becoming an active member of Sex-Aholics Anonymous. We were all so proud of him and of the miracle of sobriety for that length of time. Being the recovering pollyanna, I immediately began plans of having a five-year celebration to commemorate the end of the plague, so to speak, in our marriage. My heart wanted to be done with this scourge and to move onto bigger and better things. Enough already. Let's get this show on the road! I'm plumb tired of dealing with this...hippo.

In September of 2007, Tom failed his sobriety. While away for a month during an upgrade training in his job, he succumbed to the pressure of the voices in his head that told him "You're not enough.

You don't deserve to be captain. You will never be good enough. If only they really knew you, they would never let you be captain...." Finally, the pressure became too great. Instead of calling his sponsor and exchanging those lies for truth, he medicated with Internet porn one more time. Two hours later his sobriety and recovery were set back. The clock was pushed back to 00.01 seconds and the sobriety counting began all over again.

I wish I could say that Tom quickly called me and apologized, confessing his sins and making amends immediately after this happened. I cannot. The hardest part of Tom's "slip" as they call it in SA was that it happened in September and I didn't find out about it until November. I found out about it only because I was asking him about his upcoming five-year "sobriety" and he looked at me with that look I knew all too well.

The decision to stay or just end our marriage was one that I battled for weeks. I wrestled with it, because I had promised myself that if there was *one more time* that would be it. I finally came to a place of peace after weeks of unceasing prayer, tears, and much meditation on the Word. I knew in my heart that I was supposed to write this book and to start a ministry for other spouses just like me. I also knew that if I gave up without one more fight that Satan would win a great victory in all of our lives and that was the last thing I wanted to happen.

So, I sat Tom down and told him how sad, angry, disappointed, hurt, and "done" I was with his addiction. I felt like I had spoken my *truth*, expressing my needs without reservation, setting strong boundaries. I drew a line in the sand. No longer would I keep on trying to keep our marriage together if he wasn't going to be sold-out to his own healing and commitment (fidelity) to our marriage. It wasn't fair to me and absolutely not fair to our three wonderful daughters who were enduring the fallout from these things. The difference this time, though, was in Tom. He immediately got on the phone and called his sponsor, he immediately began going to more SA meetings. I saw in him a desire to change and to prove his commitment to our marriage by the actions he took. For me, I had spoken my truth, set boundaries, and continued doing the hard work of replacing negatives about who I am with the positives of who I am, exchanging truth for the lies.

Together, we came up with a four-phase plan that was put into place simultaneously and immediately. It was an all-out war on the enemy of our souls and our marriage and we went head and heart first into it. For the first six months, we talked, breathed, and thought of nothing more important than beginning the new habit of seeking health as a couple and individually. (Remember: it takes at least three weeks to form a new habit in your life. Recovery work is no different, and I would argue that it's even more of a challenge to change, but it is worth it and *you* are worth it!)

Phase 1: Monthly counseling/check-in with Pastor.

Phase 2: SA and sponsors for Tom every time possible.

Phase 3: Women's Support Group and a Search for Wholeness for Kolinda

Phase 4: Prayer Warriors surrounding us.

Phase 1 included incorporating one of our pastors in our story. They say "You are only as sick as your secrets." I also believe darkness loses its power when we bring it into the light. We began seeing him once a month to create a foundation of spiritual accountability for both of us. It felt good knowing that one of the shepherds of our church knew our struggles and was praying not only for Tom and me, but for each of the girls. If you attend a church that has shepherd pastors, I recommend that you keep this phase going indefinitely.

Phase 2 was for Tom to continue with his SA meetings as often as possible and with his mentors on a daily basis. This was something that Tom had already been doing and had experienced great success with already. As time passed and Tom began seeing victory in his spiritual life, he then became a sponsor to someone else in his group. God began to bless him and to challenge him with someone new in the program who called him every day. The affect on his life and walk was remarkable. No longer the new kid on the block, he was now the leader, speaking truth and holding accountable those who wanted to walk in recovery.

Phase 3 included my personal recovery and attention to emotional, physical, and spiritual health. I became a part of a women's support group that met once a week (emotional health). Next, I continued working out at the YMCA regularly and listening to my heart, not "pushing down" or ignoring my feelings (physical and emotional health). My focus was also on forgiving Tom and for trusting God to work in whatever way he wanted in our marriage—on His timetable. I made reading the Word and prayer my number one priority. (spiritual health) Was this easy? No! But I put my faith fully on God's promise to never leave or forsake and to finish the work He had begun in both of our lives. On days when I had no faith what did I do? I asked God for it and chose to keep on believing whether I felt "holy" or not! I learned that I couldn't wait to feel spiritual. God has shown me that faith requires that I choose to trust in the unseen before I ever see the fruit of my prayers and more often than not, faith requires I trust God when I see nothing in the physical realm. We are called to trust no matter what and wait on the Lord's timing, which may or may not line up with our schedules and day planners!

Phase 4 was probably the best one in my opinion. For the first time, God opened doors for others to walk alongside us and to pray for us. They were not therapists or specialists, but rather, friends and family who loved us unconditionally (that's such a great word!). This part was crucial in our healing because we knew we were not alone anymore and that helped us to remain "truthful and real." My family and my recovery friends knew our story and there was no shame! Instead of hiding our hippos, we began to say, "Hey! This is where we are and we need your prayers!" The difference we found this time was one of love and acceptance. God began to do a real work in our lives that built up our trust and love for each other.

Facing Your Hippos This Week:

Sit down with your husband this week and together, think of a plan for your recovery work. This is not an opportunity for either of you to boss the other one around and demand the other person's recovery work. Rather, this is a chance for each of you to think about what steps you are going to take so that you can become whole and healthy as individuals and as a couple. Now that you have decided you *want to be well* and have made the decision to do the hard work of becoming whole on your own, make your own list. Stick to the list and decide to do the next right thing one day at a time, expecting progress not perfection and giving each other and yourself grace along the journey!

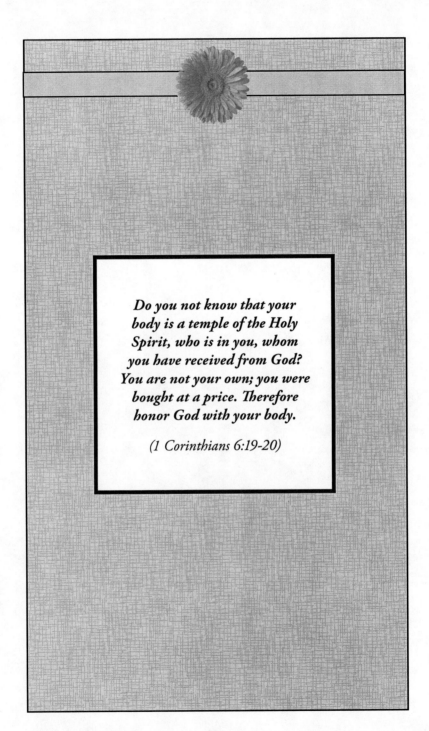

Do you not know that your body is a temple of the Holy Spirit, who is in you, whom you have received from God? You are not your own; you were bought at a price. Therefore honor God with your body.

(1 Corinthians 6:19-20)

35

TAKE GOOD CARE OF YOURSELF!

There's an old song that ends with the line, "Take good care of yourself, you belong to me!" That's actually a great slogan for all of us. One of many gifts I have received as a result of walking out of addictive strongholds is the gift of coming back to myself. I once said, "The longest road I've ever traveled is the road back to *me*." For years I blamed Tom's addiction or his work schedule or anything else that was handy for why I let myself get so run down, so tired, and so purposeless. God, in his unbelievable patience and mercy, has shown me how important this temple, my body, is. In 1 Corinthians 6:19, it states that our bodies are the temple of the living God, housing the Holy Spirit. We have been bought with a price and we are *not our own*. We belong to Jesus whose blood was shed for our eternal redemption. That's pretty amazing when you think about it.

I have learned that it's okay to spend money on myself *when I have it*. It's okay to take time away from the daily demands and process things and just rest. And, it's okay to speak my truth when I need or even want something, expressing ideas, dreams and hopes. In fact, to do all of the above-mentioned things is actually very healthy. Then, the burden of "figuring out what Kolinda's thinking" is lifted from my husband, family, and friends. No more guessing games, no more hiding the truth...no more hippos. I've learned that

I am powerless over how others respond to my requests, but I have the right and the responsibility to speak truthfully about what I need and feel. The Bible says to speak the truth in love. Through recovery, I've learned just how freeing and how beautiful this really is.

I don't know about you, but I really don't enjoy looking at old family albums. Experience has taught me that upon reflecting over past hairdos I suddenly realize just how bad a bad hair day can be. God has used the process of recovery to teach me some valuable things. Here are a few:

Okay, ladies, my Mom used to tell me that my hair is my "crowning glory." I don't spend a lot of money for manicures or pedicures, but I spend a bundle on my hair! Hair color, hair cut, hair style, hair, hair, hair! If you are limited on funds, I want to encourage you to save money each week in an envelope for your monthly haircut. I know what my haircuts cost and each week I put a fraction of that amount in a safe place so that when I am in need of some pampering, I will have the money. I have found a wonderful hairdresser who I am completely honest with so there's no guessing on her part as to what style I want! I take a picture of the cut I want so she can see it and understand where I'm coming from. Remember it's our responsibility to speak the truth to others! We've become great friends and while she helps me look better on the outside, my inside is refreshed each time I go in with lots of laughter and friendship.

Secondly, another horror I've experienced when looking over old photos is the dorky clothes I've worn on many occasions. If you have outdated clothes, try and watch a show like *What Not To Wear* where fashion experts help fashion-challenged contestants put their wardrobes together. Pick up some fashion points, save up your money, and then go and buy a new outfit! If you don't have the money, then either cut out other spending from your budget or pick up a part-time job so that you will have some "fun money" to freely spend on yourself. If you live with a spouse who isn't being honest with you about his addiction or his infidelity, it can honestly make you feel insane and before you know it, if you don't take care of yourself, you'll find yourself enmeshed in the craziness that comes with sexual addiction and any addiction for that matter. By realizing the importance of taking care of our physical and emotional needs, we begin to take back who we are and the healing process begins. One of my favorite verses from the Bible is "All beautiful you are, my darling; there is no flaw in you" (Song of Songs, 4:7). This verse speaks to all of us "brides of Christ" who long to hear we are *beautiful* in our Father's eyes. And we are – whether anyone verbalizes that to us or not. It's a fact!

Another area where we can honor our bodies as the "temple of the Holy Spirit" is by making sure that we know ourselves well enough to insure that we don't become unbalanced emotionally or physically. If we need some medication for depression, we make the call to the doctor, set and keep the appointment, and get the help we need. If we need some multi-vitamins for women to keep our physical bodies at their peak, we either find a holistic doctor or visit our friendly neighborhood health food store and get the help we need. If we need to talk to a friend who perhaps has offended us, we find the courage within ourselves through prayer and with a praying friend's help to speak our truth to the offending person so that we are healthy emotionally. We do this in order to live at peace with others and ourselves and to restore balance to our bodies.

I've mentioned earlier the importance of spending time in prayer and reading God's Word for our spiritual health each day. One of the greatest benefits of aging that I've discovered so far is that I have learned to say, "No!" I remember times when the girls were very young when I felt like if I didn't do it all...well, the church would have to close its doors! The truth is, God is more than capable of finding someone to fill my spot if I'll just get my big, bad self out of the way. When I am choosing to spend time each day in the Word and am willing to surrender my agenda to His agenda for my life, then I will be more willing to say yes to the eternal things and no to those things of lesser importance. There are tons of good things to do in life. The question is "What is the BEST thing?" God promises that His plans for us are for the good and not to harm us. If I am listening to His voice and not my own performance driven desires, I will make the right choices.

He has taught me that if my day-planner is too overbooked, then I need to graciously bow out. I've learned, first of all, *to think before I commit to anything* and, secondly, if I have to quit something, to apologize for any inconvenience and explain (with no shame or guilt) that at this time in my life I need to go in a different direction. I make amends, I speak my truth, and then I go on with what I know God is calling me to do! It's that simple, and, let me tell you, it's so liberating!

There's an old story that my husband has told me several times. The flight attendants are taught in their training to tell the passengers, "In case of an emergency, put your oxygen mask on *first*. Then, and only then, will you be able to help others around you in need." You see, if we who are wives of sex addicts (whether they are in recovery or not) don't take care of our own emotional, spiritual, and physical needs first, then we will never be able to care for our families and others in a healthy way. Remember: doing the *hard work* on our own really is worth it!

 Facing Your Hippos This Week:

Okay, now here's your homework for this week. As hard as this will probably be for a lot of you wonderful women, ask yourself, "What is one thing I would like to do for myself this week?" Then, look at your calendars or day planners and make the time to do just *one* thing for yourself this coming week. No excuses!!! Some examples may be:

1. When your kids go to school, curl up on the couch for one hour with your favorite book.
2. When your husband gets home from work one night this week ask him to take care of the kids while you fill up your bathtub, light some candles, put on Michael Buble's CD and soak in some fragrant bubbles for as long as you can stand it!
3. Make yourself a cup of hot, green tea or pour yourself a glass of wine. Put on your favorite pajamas by early evening or leave them on in the morning, and watch an hour of your favorite TV show.
4. Draw a picture.
5. Go outside and take some pictures of the spring flowers or the fall foliage.

6. Walk the dog.
7. Have a lunch date with a friend.
8. Go to the mall and just walk around, getting ideas.
9. Call a friend.
10. Work out with your favorite CD or go to the gym.

*Therefore, as God's chosen people,
holy and dearly loved, clothe
yourselves with compassion,
kindness, humility, gentleness and
patience. Bear with each other
and forgive whatever grievances
you may have against one another.
Forgive as the LORD forgave
you. And over all these virtues
put on love, which binds them
all together in perfect unity.*

(Colossians 3:12-14)

36

COURAGE IN THE FACE OF HIPPOS

October 29, 2008
Dear Kolinda,

When we married on September 6, 1986, I know it was your deeply held dream and intention that it was to be for as long as we both should live. You also expected us to be devoted exclusively to each other in mind, body, emotion and spirit. I know that you have held true to that and have been faithful to your vows and faithful to me.

You deserved the same from me and should have received that, but I failed you. I sinned against you and against God for being unfaithful to you. For that I am deeply sorry.

I took in the pictures of pornography and gave myself away to images and fantasies. Early in our marriage, I also got too close emotionally to other acquaintances in ...(Germany, Arkansas, Minnesota, Florida) I should have given all of myself exclusively to you. My addiction has not only hurt our marriage but has hurt our family. Our three girls have felt the repercussions from my sins and I'm sure it has affected them. This has added to the efforts you have needed to raise and parent them as a mother. Without my addiction, there wouldn't have been these extra issues you have had to deal with.

My unfaithfulness has affected other relationships in our lives. You've had to deal with awkwardness, misunderstandings, and embarrassments with friends and other church members: the small group in Minnesota being one example.

Once again, I am truly sorry for all the hurt, pain, and broken promises I have caused you and done to you. I hope to begin and continue to make amends to you by living a changed life and by finally being faithful to our marriage vows. I pledge to you my complete love and complete devotion.

Tom

As you can see from the date, Tom wrote this letter to me in October of 2008. The obvious sincerity and repentance in his words was something I longed for and honestly needed in order for the trust in our marriage to begin the long road of restoration. For the first two to three years of Tom's recovery, I had a critical spirit of him and really battled with totally trusting that he was sorry and that he was really going to change. I struggled with a lot of fear and huge doubts. Trust was not my companion, really it was an elusive mirage to me. I longed for it, but after so many years of seeing the cycle of his addiction and my enabling of it, I was skeptical that lasting change was possible. After we attended some recovery workshops, as his "homework," Tom would apologize. I longed for a spontaneous apology but until he wrote this letter, it never came.

By 2008, thankfully and in God's perfect timing, both of us had come a long way in our growth both spiritually and emotionally. God had been working and reshaping both of our hearts, revealing to me the crucial need of forgiving him 100% in order to move on in light of Christ and of Tom's obvious efforts to remain sober.

As I said before, living with someone who has struggled with a sexual addiction is not an easy thing for either person in the couple ship. The difference in a spouse who is committed to a marriage and who is working on recovery will be seen in the day to day. When an addict really wants to walk in the freedom that Christ can bring and chooses to seek God and to change, the wife will be the beneficiary of his efforts!

It was not more than a month after he wrote the above-mentioned letter that Tom came home and told me he had flirted inappropriately with a flight attendant on a trip the week prior. He recognized his behavior, stopped it and then repented of it, all because he realized that his emotions were going in the wrong direction. Nothing happened. In fact, most men wouldn't have even mentioned it. I remember feeling hurt, sadness but mostly gladness all at the same time as Tom had told me the truth. I saw how God was working in his heart and that Tom was listening to the Holy Spirit and to his own heart. By recognizing the behavior and stopping it *before* his mind or actions went any further and then by seeking to honestly confess it to me meant so much. For me, it proved his desire to remain true to our marriage vows and it was inspiring to me as I saw Tom making godly choices. I was so proud of him and I quickly told him so!

When Satan comes a knockin', I am learning to recognize the attack that is aimed at dismantling my marriage vows and I face it. You see, for the rest of my time on this earth, I know temptations will come both for Tom and for me. The choice we both must make will be whether or not we want to do what Jesus would have us to do or to serve temporal things. I am thankful for groups like Sexaholics Anonymous (S.A.) and Women of Restoration that allow men and women to come and share their hearts in a safe and encouraging environment. When the hippos come, and they will, I pray Tom and I will be ready as we daily prepare our hearts, minds and souls.

 ## Facing Your Hippos This Week:

The reality of living with a recovering addict to pornography is that your husband will face times of testing. So will you. James 1:2 says, "Consider it pure joy, my brothers (and sisters), whenever you face trials of many kinds..." It doesn't say IF you face trials of many kinds. It says *whenever* you face trials. We WILL be tempted and we WILL face trials. The difference between victory and failure in our Christian walk is in our response to the temptation and trial. This week as you spend time with the LORD in prayer and meditating on His word, write down verses that talk about victory, strength and power. (Remember to look in the back of your Bible under the concordance for help.) We are "hard pressed on every side." But we are NOT defeated!

Don't let anyone look down on you because you are young, but set an example for the believers in speech, in life, in love, in faith and in purity.

(1 Timothy 4:12)

37
SAFE HAVEN

My prayer in writing this book is for women in similar situations who can find hope and healing through my story and the resources that have proven to work in my marriage. God has broken my heart over the issue of pornography as I know it breaks His heart to see His creation distorting the perfect plan He intended for sex. In marriage, it is the most beautiful act one person can share with another, in commitment and trust. Pornography takes what was meant for our good, for pleasure and for fulfillment and twists and corrupts it so that women *and men* are seen as nothing more than objects, things to be used over and over again without any regard to the person's heart, soul or worth.

The issue of sexual addiction is complicated and touches not only the addict to pornography but also the wife and family in ways that are immeasurable. I have heard in the recovery world phrases like "Oh, your husband has wounds and that's why he did what he did." "It's not about you. It's his problem. You need to focus on all of your shortcomings and let him work his program without any intervention on your part." While there is some truth in these comments, there is a greater truth that I wish the world could hear. That truth is that sexual addiction is unlike the other addictions because it affects the wife who is in a covenant relationship with her husband. It is not like the alcoholic who drinks a drink or the drug addict who takes a hit. Yes, the drink and drug affect the relationship of the spouse but it is not in the same way that the wife of a sex addict feels. When a man looks at pornography and violates the covenant relationship he has made between himself, his wife and God, there is something sacred that is broken. This is like humpty dumpty and when that trust is broken, it is impossible to completely put the pieces back together again. Something is lost, broken and will never quite be the same again.

When I tried to share our story with some of the small group in Minnesota and seek help by exposing our secret, I did so because I was desperate to find answers. I longed, like I believe many other women in the church, for someone to listen and to show up in our lives who could understand the pain of the addiction we were facing. I didn't find it until 2008. By God's sovereign plan, I heard about a women's confidential support group that met in a local church. As soon as I could, I began attending. For the first time in my life, I found a group of likeminded women who loved me unconditionally and who extended that grace and care to me. It was like a long awaited prayer being answered and a huge, healing breath of fresh air that filled my long deflated lungs to capacity!

After about a year of attending a weekly meeting and learning how to "feel" and share my feelings, I began feeling like the Lord wanted me to bring a similar type of group to the Baptist church I was attending. Nothing existed like it and I felt a burden to at least offer the ministry. In January of 2009, Safe Haven was launched and from the beginning, I knew God's hand was upon the women who came. The number of courageous women was small, but the quality was great. Each brought something special that the rest needed. In November of that same year, a second group began meeting in my home. We shared our stories, laughed together, risked being vulnerable with our true feelings and always ended the meeting with a word of support and challenge to rise above our circumstances. My goal in both groups has been and continues to be to work on becoming whole on our own.

Harvest:

Almost six years have passed since Tom and I told each of our daughters our story, exposing the reality of the hippos in our home. I have to admit that when our counselor first recommended we do so, I went along with the idea kicking and screaming. After all, I had spent so much of my time and energy trying to hide the darn hippos in our lives.

Six years of Tom's journey of sobriety and of turning over a new leaf, of flipping it over, of trying to be honest and open about our struggles both with each other, with our girls and with others. As parents, there aren't any guarantees that we are doing anything right, or if anything we are trying so desperately to pound into our children's heads is going to stick or make any kind of lasting difference. But, God is good and as always, He has given us glimpses of His redemption at just the right times in our marriage.

One particular Sunday morning our women's ministry director asked me to stand by the Safe Haven banner in the front lobby of our church. It was between the services when some of the wonderful ladies who attend the group started coming up and chatting. We were having a mini family reunion of sorts and I was lovin' it! My youngest daughter, Tom and two of the husbands whose wives attend Safe Haven had gathered by the large spiral stairway near the foyer. They were making small talk.

My youngest daughter was sitting in the midst of this crowd of recovering addicts, her daddy by her side. In the conversation, one of them mentioned that he attended a Celebrate Recovery program that another local church offered. My daughter turned innocently to her father and said, "Where do you go, Dad?" Tom went on to say without any shame and without missing a beat that he attends a SA group in Franklin.

When my friend and her husband who had been listening to our daughter got in their car to go home, he turned to her and asked, "Do Tom's girls *know* about his addiction??" My friend smiled and said, "Yeah, they do. Isn't that neat how their family lives in honesty. Nothing is hidden. They all know." My friend told me how her husband couldn't believe this. How his father, even now at the age of 70, STILL looks at porn and no one, including his knowing wife, thinks it is wrong.

When this story got back to me via my friend, I cried tears of joy. For the first time, I really saw how God in His providence was redeeming our family from this addiction thing. He was stopping generational curses of repressed feelings, insufficient affection and codependency in his family line as I was confronting codependent traits in mine. What once held us in bondage was losing its stronghold! I could see clearly the importance of walking in truth, because our children needed it more than anything and others who are watching our lives needed to see how God could redeem anything, including sexual addiction.

How different our family is from when we first moved to Tennessee! Here we were all standing in a church foyer with others who were walking testimonies of God's victory. Oh, how our lives had changed for the better! No more toxic shame. No more hiding our hippos! No more exhaustive attempts to be something we are not, just honest transparency and freedom that comes from surrendering our stuff to a God who is big enough to handle every situation far better than we could ever dream or even imagine.

God has taught me that my "job" as a Christian wife is to love my husband enough to surrender him to God's capable care. That means I pray for Tom every day and especially when he is on his trips to remain true to his marriage vows, but most of all to remain truest to his God, his faith and his commitment to Jesus Christ. I surrender him to the Lord and use my energies and time to work on my own relationship with God. As each of us works on our own spiritual, emotional and physical health, we are then equipped to love each other in a healthy way and to share that love with others.

We've been working this recovery program now for almost 7 years and to be honest, a whole lot of things have changed in our house. I no longer dream of the cottage with the white picket fence nor do I expect Tom to rescue me on his white horse from all of the evils of this life. Instead, through our journey, God has taught me of *His* sufficiency and *His* abundant grace that are enough to meet all of my Grand Canyon sized needs. I have learned to take one day at a time with my Sweet Jesus and to leave the perfectionistic expectations behind while looking upward and inward for life's answers. We will always have hippos that want to come into our home. The difference now is that both Tom and I recognize them, call them out by name and are no longer afraid to face them. Oh, they may come, but we don't hide them anymore nor do we cower in fear if they snap their jaws at us. I am grateful to God for using Tom's addiction and my codependency to teach us to look to Him alone for our completeness. I couldn't do life very well without Jesus before recovery work. Now that I have walked through so much with my husband, I don't want to do life without Jesus. And, for the first time in my life, I can honestly tell you that I have found the answer to my problems and HE is big enough, sufficient enough and patient enough to see me through whatever comes my way.

To God be the glory for GREAT THINGS He has done!

Safe Haven Testimonials:

Safe Haven: A gift from God at a time when my life was completely shattered. It was on May 5, 2008 that my life was devastated. My life was surrounded by plans for retirement and looking forward to those wonderful golden years with my loving husband and best friend. I had been faithfully married 43.5 years to my high school sweetheart, lover and lifetime soul mate. Unfortunately, on this day, my husband told me that he would rather die than hurt me with what he was about to say. Then, he told me that he was really sick and had a sexual addiction. He had been unfaithful to me and tried to tell me he had never loved anyone else but me. He had gone from pornography, to phone sex to actively being with numerous call girls and prostitutes. My entire life was shattered with his words. Why and how, dear God, could this have happened? I thought we loved each other deeply. Our love life was great. How could I have not seen this? The shock was more than I could bear. I can't begin to explain what went on in my mind or body. I also found that I had been infected with an STD.

In January of 2009, my daughter handed me a brochure from our church called Safe Haven. It described a confidential support group for wives whose husbands struggle with these issues. My husband had been involved in all of these. I held the brochure in my hand and made the call to find out more about the group. I started attending and continue to be an active member. If it weren't for Safe Haven, I would still be "spinning" and would not know how to deal with all of the feelings associated with this situation. I do see Safe Haven as a gift from God. (S.)

I would say the thing that pops into my head is the relief that you are not alone- the name Safe Haven-sounded like such a perfect name when I heard it....I think this group is and will become a place of learning and growing and healing. I like that the focus is on our recovery- and learning that we are all hurting people- and that our feelings help us unlock the pain that keep us from enjoying a full life – the life that Christ wants for each of us. I look forward to growing and learning who I am in Christ. (M.)

What an amazing ride life has been! Being part of Safe Haven has been life-changing. For the first time in my life, I am getting "my life back." Realizing that I have choices. Not to feel "powerless" or stuck as I would have described my circumstances for the past twenty-four years. God bless you, for starting this group and for your obedience! (D.)

I have learned to recognize my feelings, accept them and learned to ask God to meet me in them. (Chip Dodd Feelings Chart: Anger, Hurt, Lonely, Afraid, Sad, Guilt, Shame and Glad). (Anonymous)

Coming to Safe Haven has helped me to be STRONG in the Lord, helping me to know that no matter what comes my way in this life, Christ will hold me. (Anonymous)

The most positive thing I have gained from coming weekly to Safe Haven is that I am now walking with others who know and understand sexual addiction and who share my faith. (Anonymous)

38
MY PRAYER FOR YOU

I pray, dear Jesus, for every woman who is just like me: married to a man who is struggling with the stronghold of pornography and seeking answers, wanting her life to be at a better and healthier place. I pray, Father, that You would help her know that You are her Heavenly Husband, her best and most trustworthy friend and that she is not alone. Help her to know she has an advocate in Heaven who knows her intimately and who calls her by name. Help her to rest in your promises and to daily allow You to fill up all her "empty places" with the Living Water of your Holy Spirit. Let that abundance overflow into every facet of her life. Lift her up above her circumstances to see just how good You are and just how much You love her, Lord. Help her to start living each day by putting You first and by trusting in Your abundant GRACE.

Holy, holy, holy are You, Lord God Almighty, who was and is and is yet to come. I praise You for who You are and for who You have proven Yourself to be in my life. Thank You, Lord, for meeting our every need and for never leaving us alone. Help my sister to know these truths right now and it is in Jesus' mighty name that is above all circumstances and most of all, all addictions and co-dependencies,

I pray.
AMEN

Part 3: Resource List

Resources

www.safehaven4women.com
safehaven4women@gmail.com

**A Word of Encouragement for you: As you begin to walk on the path of finding hope, I want to encourage you to read some of the books below. I have listed them in the order that I read them, but you may find that there is one that the Holy Spirit especially points you to read. Please do so! I am praying for you as you begin this journey and I want you to know: YOU ARE NOT ALONE!

Books

1. **Serenity Bible Companion for 12-Step Recovery,** Dr. Robert Hemfelt and Dr. Richard Fowler. Thomas Nelson Publishers

2. **The Confident Woman**, Anabel Gillham. Harvest House Publishers

3. **Codependent No More**, Melody Beattie. Hazelden Publishers

4. **Beyond Codependency, And Getting Better All The Time**, Melody Beattie. Hazelden Publishers

5. **Secret Wars, Living with Your Husband's Secret Wars**, Marsha Means. Revell Publishing

6. **Shattered Vows**, Debra Laaser. Zondervan

7. **The Voice of the Heart, A Call to Full Living**, Chip Dodd. Providence House Publishers

8. **Jesus Calling**, Sarah Young - Devotional

9. **Streams in the Desert**, E.B. Cowan - Devotional

10. **Reflections of Hope** (S-Anon)

11. **Celebrate Recovery Bible**, Zondervan

12. **Lord, I want to know You**, Kay Arthur. Waterbrook Press

Books to help in understanding sexual addiction -

1. **Faithful & True: Sexual Integrity In A Fallen World**, Mark Laaser, Ph.D.

2. **False Intimacy, Understanding the Struggle of Sexual Addiction**, Dr. Harry. W. Schaumburg

3. **The Pornography Trap**, Ralph H. Earle Jr. and Mark R. Laaser

4. **Healing Wounds of Sexual Addiction**, Mark Laaser, Ph.D.

5. **Don't Call It Love**, Patrick Carnes

CDs

Somebody's Daughter, Confronting the Lies of Pornography
www.musicforthesoul.org

Counselors Specializing in Sexual Addiction Recovery

Center for Relational Healing
Lisa Gohmann, Ken Graham - 7003 Chadwick Dr. Suite 258
Brentwood, TN/37027 - www.relationalhealing.com
615-377-8866 (Ken)
615-400-6577 (Lisa)

Chip Dodd - www.sagehillresources.com 877-861-1170

Internet Filtering Software

www.covenanteyes.com

www.besecure.com

www.InternetSafety.com (Site for Safe Eyes)

www.MyInternetDoorman.com

www.NetNanny.com

www.seenoevilonline.com

Ministries:

Faithful and True Ministries, Inc. - Mark and Debra Laaser
15798 Venture Lane
Eden Prairie, MN 55344
www.faithfulandtrueministries.com

Holy Homes - Clay and Renee Cross
PO Box 565
Arlington, TN 38002
www.holyhomes.org/home

Restore Ministries
***Check your local YMCA for details

1. Journey to Freedom - Scott Reall

2. Power to Choose (Twelve Steps to Freedom) - Mike O'Neil

3. Love Is A Choice (Freedom in Relationships) - Dr. Robert Hemfelt, Dr. Frank Minirth, Dr. Paul Meier, Dr. Deborah Newman and Dr. Brian Newman

Online Recovery Websites:

www.candeocan.com - An online pornography addiction recovery training and coaching program. Dr. Randy Hyde, licensed clinical psychologist, Dr. Bernell Christiansen, licensed marriage and family therapist

www.freedombeginshere.org

Support Groups:

Celebrate Recovery – www.celebraterecovery.com

Codependents Anonymous
PO Box 33577
Phoenix, AZ 85067-3577
602.277.7991
www.codependents.org

Codependents of Sex Addicts (COSA)
PO Box 14537
Minneapolis, MN 55414
763.537.6904
www.cosa-recovery.org

S-Anon
PO Box 111242
Nashville, TN 37222-1242
615.833.3152
www.sanon.org

Safe Haven – Confidential Women's Support Group - Brentwood Baptist Church, Brentwood, TN **Meets on Thursday mornings from 9:30 to 11:30 in Brentwood and also in the Spring Hill/Thompson Station area of TN on Tuesday nights from 6:30 to 8:30.
www.safehaven4women.com

Women of Restoration - Fellowship Bible Church, Franklin, TN
**Meets on Monday Nights at 6:30 p.m.
Contact Colleen Hoagland at 615.300.7248

Workshops:

Bethesda Workshops, Marnie Ferree
3710 Franklin Rd.
Nashville, TN 37204
www.bethesdaworkshops.org

LaVergne, TN USA
08 October 2010
200131LV00002B/2/P